BUILD YOUR OWN
IBM®
COMPATIBLE AND
SAVE A BUNDLE

No. 2831
$22.95

BUILD YOUR OWN
IBM®
COMPATIBLE AND
SAVE A BUNDLE

AUBREY PILGRIM

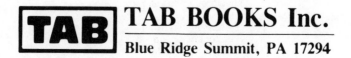

TAB BOOKS Inc.

Blue Ridge Summit, PA 17294

Dedication:
To the memory of
my wife

FIRST EDITION

THIRD PRINTING

Printed in the United States of America

Library of Congress Cataloging in Publication Data

Pilgrim, Aubrey.
Build your own IBM compatible and save a bundle.

Includes index.
1. Microcomputers—Design and construction—
Amateurs' manuals. I. Title.
TK9969.P55 1987   621.391'6   86-23111
ISBN 0-8306-0231-3
ISBN 0-8306-2831-2 (pbk.)

Questions regarding the content of this book
should be addressed to:

Reader Inquiry Branch
Editorial Department
TAB BOOKS Inc.
Blue Ridge Summit, PA 17294

Contents

Acknowledgment

Computers were furnished for photographs by the Paramount Electronics Company, 1155 Tasman Drive, Sunnyvale, CA 94089.

Introduction

You may not believe this, but in this computer era, there are still some people who say, "Why do I need a computer? What would I use it for?" No doubt there were similar people back in the caveman days who said, "Why do we need the wheel?"

WHY YOU NEED A COMPUTER

The computer is still in its infancy, less than a decade old as we know it today. Yet it has already made thousands of things possible in science, industry, and technology that weren't even dreamed of a few years ago. It has enhanced and made the life of every one of us better in countless ways. Because of the computer we have more leisure time, more luxuries, better health, and a better society. But even the most sophisticated computer that we have today is crude and primitive compared to those that will be developed in the next few years.

Yet some people still ask, "What can a computer do for me personally?" Here is a short list of things that you can do with a computer. It is by no means complete.

Word Processing. Every person has an innate creative instinct of some sort. Writing is one of the most creative acts there is. Who knows, maybe there lurks within you the ability to write a great American novel. With a word processor, you can juggle sentences, paragraphs or pages around until they are just right, then print them out. For example, I just came back from the end of this chapter and added these last two sentences.

My handwriting is so bad that not even I can read it when it gets cold. I can't type very well either. I have used gallons of white-out covering up errors that I have made on a typewriter. With a computer, I can go back and type over my errors, and when the text is perfect, I can print it out. If your handwriting is as bad as mine, you need a computer just to write letters. You could then write legible letters to your rich uncle and other relatives and friends. You could write letters of complaint to the president of the company that sold you that piece of high-priced shoddy merchandise. Or you could use your computer to write nasty letters to the editor of your local paper, or to your congressman.

Many people can't spell very well. Spelling is not a measure of intelligence, but if you write a report, a memo or a letter that has misspelled words, people will just automatically think you are dumb. Many of the word processors, such as WordStar, have spelling checkers. There are also thesaurus programs, such as Wordfinder, that can help you choose the right words. RIGHTWRITER is another excellent tool for anyone who writes. It can analyze a document for errors in grammar, punctuation, usage and style. Just these three programs are reason enough to justify owning a computer.

Home Finances. You could use a computer to keep track of all your expenses, keep track of your checks, and balance your checkbook. There are software programs that can help you formulate a good budget and help you manage your money.

Home Banking. There are many banks now who will let you do all of your banking from home with a computer and a modem. You would no longer have to drive downtown, hunt for a parking space, then stand in a long line just to make a simple transfer.

Income Taxes. Our income tax laws are so complicated and complex that many people have to hire someone else to do their returns. There are many good tax software programs that you can use to do your own income taxes. In the near future, the Internal Revenue Service will probably allow you to use a modem to feed your tax return directly from your computer into theirs. Some large, professional tax preparers are doing this already.

On-Line Services. With a home computer and a modem, there are several services that are available to you. You can shop by computer from home, view air line schedules, or real-time stock market quotations, or access many other large database services.

Bulletin Boards. With a computer and a modem, you can access hundreds of bulletin boards over the telephone lines. You can use a modem to chat with other hackers, leave messages, or download *public domain* or *shareware* software. There are hundreds of software programs on these bulletin boards. Many of these programs are as good or better than some equivalent programs that cost $300.00 to $400.00. Public domain programs cost only the time it takes to download them into your system. The shareware programs include a message requesting that you make a small donation if you like the program. Although you do not have to pay it, it is to everyone's benefit if you do. This supports public domain software, and undercuts the big corporations who sell copy-protected programs for hundreds of dollars more than their production costs. You may also purchase public domain software from other sources for a cost of $3.00 to $10.00. See the Appendix for a source listing.

Family Records. You could use your computer to store all of your family records of births, marriages, deaths and other important dates. You could do some research and build up your family tree. But you should be aware that if you search too diligently, you may find a monkey in that tree.

Other Records. If you are an audiophile, you could have a database of all your records or tapes, with a listing of each one by artist, date, and any other pertinent information.

Addresses. You could have an address and telephone listing of friends, businesses, and relatives. There are software programs that will print out the addresses on envelopes, or dial telephone numbers for you.

Serial Numbers. You could make a listing of serial numbers and descriptions of all of your expensive items. This might include items such as your video recorder, television set, cameras, computer and peripherals and anything else of value in your house. This will make the police department and your insurance agent very happy in case you ever get burglarized. Note: Put the listing on a floppy diskette and hide it so that the burglar can't steal that also.

Recipes. If you are tired of the same old thing every night, there are several software packages with hundreds of good recipes. And of course you can always add your own favorites.

Games. There are hundreds of software programs that will let you play all kinds of games on your computer. There are arcade type games, chess, checkers, football, baseball, hockey, dice, blackjack, solitaire and hundreds of others. There are many public domain games that are free from bulletin boards.

Bowling Scores. If you belong to a bowling league or some other club, a computer is ideal for keeping scores of all the participants. A computer can also be used to publish newsletters for club members, keep financial records and all kinds of other data. If you belong to a club, take up a collection, hold a raffle, increase the dues and buy a computer for the club.

Sporting Odds. If you are a betting person, there are programs that can help you pick the best horse. Or figure the odds on a football game and other events. These programs can give you a slight edge, but you should be aware that any such program may be somewhat less than perfect. So don't bet the rent.

Stocks and Bonds. If you know what you are doing, you can make a lot of money in the stock market. There are several programs that can help you make better investments.

Computers at Work. If you work in any kind of business or industry, there will be computers connected with it in some way. No matter what your job is, if you know a little bit about computers, you will be able to do it better. You might even be able to convince your boss to give you a promotion and a raise.

Educational. Computers are excellent for teaching both children and adults. You can learn math, reading, especially rapid reading, grammar, foreign languages, typing and almost any other subject with the help of a computer. You can even use a computer to learn about computers.

Legal Needs. There are some very good programs on floppy diskettes that will allow you to make up your own will. You could print up a copy of it and leave it lying around for would-be heirs to see. And if they don't start treating you right, then you can change the will in an instant.

There are also software programs for other legal needs, such as rental contracts, and other minor legal needs. These programs cannot entirely replace a good lawyer, but they are great for minor legal needs. They can save you a lot of time. And if your lawyer charges you $50.00 just to say hello on the phone, it could save you a bit of money too.

Health and Nutrition. There are several good diet and nutrition software programs that are available for home computers. They can help you plan your meals and create your own diet.

There are also programs that can help you play doctor. Some programs list all the drugs, indications and contraindications for their use, effects and side effects. On others you can input your symptoms and they will give you a list of possible diagnoses.

These programs cannot take the place of a good doctor. But they could save the time and money that you might spend going to a doctor for a minor ailment that you could take care of yourself.

Programs like this are ideal for hypochondriacs. If you have a friend who has just about exhausted all of the common maladies that he thinks he has, one of these programs could give him enough material to last several lifetimes.

There are even programs that can help with sexual problems. Sex is very important to all of us. Where would we be without it? A computer program called Intracourse asks a lot of personal questions about your private sex life that you probably wouldn't discuss even with a therapist. In case you are very innocent it has a large dictionary of dirty words and explains what they mean. From the answers to the questions it asks, an analysis of your sex life is created. It then offers some suggestions that could help. It can't take the place of a good sex therapist, but it can help. It is kind of fun just to run the program and give different answers to the questions.

Teachers. Being a teacher involves a lot of work outside the classroom, including making up class schedules, making up tests, grading papers, keeping a record of grades and attendance, and many other tasks. A computer can be a tremendous help. I definitely needed one when I was teaching. But they were still very expensive in 1980, and teachers don't make a lot of money.

Preachers. It can take a lot of time to research and write a Sunday sermon. There are software programs that have the Bible on diskette. A word, a phrase or any part of the Bible can be instantly called up and viewed.

Musicians. Much of the music created and recorded today is done with the help of a computer. It is a natural for storing and creating many new sounds, and it can be done at the touch of a keyboard key. If only Bach and Beethoven were around today.

Computing Instead of Commuting. There are many jobs that can be done just as well at home on a computer as at work in an office. Many people are hooking up to the office with a modem and doing their jobs at home. You may even do your work on a floppy disk or with a portable computer at home, then take it in to work once in a while.

This is an ideal solution for women who have small children or need to stay home for some other reason.

It might also be beneficial to your health. There are more people killed each year on our highways than were killed in ten years during the Vietnam War.

Computers for the Kids. If you have young children and you have not yet bought a computer for them, there is no excuse for not buying one now. As you well know, it is a tough world. You need all the breaks you can get. If your kids know a little bit about computers, it might give them a little bit of an edge.

Many parents will go out and buy an Apple, a Commodore or an Atari for their kids. But you can put together an IBM compatible starter system for less than what one of those toys would cost. If you are short of money, you can buy a few components as you can afford them, then put them together later. Maybe you could even let the kids help you put it together. It would be a great learning experience.

Other Reasons for Computers. There are hundreds of other reasons for computers. Repair shops, dairy farmers, realtors, photographers, doctors, dentists, lawyers, truckers, the butcher, the baker, the candlestick maker, and even the old dirt farmer all need computers. These are only a few of the people who need computers. The list could go on and on. Almost every individual, and all businesses, whether big, small, or in between, can benefit to some extent from this excellent tool.

BUILDING YOUR OWN COMPATIBLE: NO EXPERTISE REQUIRED

It is not necessary to be an electronics engineer to be able to assemble a PC clone or to upgrade an IBM computer. Even if you don't know a ROM from a RAM or a RAM from a ewe, you can still do it. If you know which end of a screwdriver to use, then you shouldn't have too much trouble. And you don't have to be a programmer in order to use a computer. There are many excellent off-the-shelf programs that will do almost anything that you could possibly want.

The first two chapters of this book will tell you what you need and where to get it. Chapters three and four are where the fun begins. In those chapters you are actually led through the assembly of an XT clone and an AT clone. Chapter five shows you the many ways in which your old IBM can be upgraded. The next eight chapters will tell you about each of the main components and accessories for your computer. After that, Chapter 14 offers troubleshooting tips. Finally, there are some chapters on DOS, other software, computer furniture, manuals, and computer swaps. The glossary in the back will help you with any unfamiliar terms. Now it's time to begin on your way to powerful, but inexpensive computing.

A WARNING

I think I should warn you that if you turn out to be a true hacker, you will never have a completed system. There will always be other pieces of hardware, software and goodies that you must have for your computer. It is like an addiction. Computer junkies will do almost anything to get their "fix." They may neglect to pay the rent or let the wife and kids go without shoes. It is very easy to become hooked, so please consider carefully before you proceed. Don't say that you weren't warned.

Chapter 1

What You Need To Build an IBM Compatible Computer

You can easily assemble your own PC-XT or PC-AT computer that will be faster, more powerful and have more functions than the best configured IBM Personal Computer. And you can do it for about half the cost of an equivalent IBM computer.

If you are not familiar with the innards of a computer you may be afraid to tackle a job like this. There are many engineers who know a lot about electronics, but have had very little experience with the insides of computers, so some of them hesitate to build their own.

But I assure you that you won't need to know anything at all about electronics and you won't have to do any wiring or soldering. The only tools you will need are a pair of pliers and a couple of screwdrivers. It takes just two or three hours to mount the main components into the case. Then just plug in the cables and boards and you can save up to $3000.00 or even more over the cost of an equivalent IBM PC-XT or AT.

Your computer will look very much like the IBM except that it won't have the IBM logo. In addition to costing less, your computer could have more functions and capabilities than the highest priced IBM-PC XT or PC-AT.

MINIMUM NEEDS FOR A BAREBONES SYSTEM

We know that you are anxious to get started so here is a list of the components that you will need for a barebones system: a case, a mother board, a power supply, one or two floppy disk drives, a disk drive controller card, a printer card, a monitor card, a color or monochrome monitor, and a keyboard. This will get you up and running. Of course you might also want to add a hard disk and its controller card, a multifunction card with extra memory, a printer, or a modem. We will discuss each of these components in detail in later chapters.

Here is just a brief description and some recommendations for each:

Case. There are several styles available. I would suggest the flip top because it makes installing or changing an expansion board much easier.

Mother Board. The mother board is one of the most important components of the system. By all means get one that will accept 640 K of on-board memory. The optional or switchable 8 MHz turbo capability is also worth a little extra money. You should make sure that it has a four layer circuit board. If possible, have the vendor install an 8088-2 or NEC V20 CPU chip for 8 MHz operations.

Power Supply. The power supply should be at least 135 watts. If you can find one for about the same price, you might even buy a 150 watt supply. You might have trouble fitting anything larger in the space available.

Floppy Drives. Try to find a fairly well known brand of half-height drives. You can get by fairly well with a single drive. If you only have one, the computer will call it drive A: and drive B: It will be able to copy a diskette from A: to B: by reading the data from the first diskette into memory. Then when that diskette is removed and a new one inserted, the data in memory will be written on it.

I would suggest that you buy a single floppy and a 20 Mb hard disk drive, or at least two floppies to save you the trouble of switching disks.

Floppy Disk Controller. Most of the controller boards for the XT can control two internal drives and two external drives. These cards have an edge connector on the front of the card and a 37 pin D type connector on the rear. Some of the clones do not have the connector for the second set of drives. You may never need the external drives, but you never know. There are some high density drives that can be connected to this connector and several tape backup systems use it. I would insist on the one that can control four floppies.

The PC and XT floppy and hard disk controller cards will work in an AT, but the AT normally uses a controller that can control both the high density 1.2 Mb floppy drive, the 360 K drive and one or two hard disks.

Printer Card. You may not have to buy this card separately. Most printers sold today are of the parallel type. But there are still some serial types sold. If you buy an external modem, you will need a serial port. Many of the multifunction boards have both a parallel and serial port. Some of the monitor boards also have a printer port.

Monitor Card. Whether you buy a monochrome or color monitor will determine which card you will need. The monochrome card is a bit more expensive, but it gives higher resolution. Unfortunately, monochrome cards are not capable of displaying colors. For that, you will need a Color Graphics Adapter, or CGA, which will give you four colors. If you can afford it, by all means buy a high resolution monitor and an Enhanced Graphics Adapter (EGA) to go with it. These will give you better resolution, plus graphics in 16 colors. The original IBM EGA cost about $1000.00. You can now buy a clone for about $200.00.

Monitor. If you are short of money, you can get a fairly good monochrome monitor for about $100.00. You can get a fairly good color monitor for about $250.00. If at all possible, I would buy a color monitor. Colors help to brighten the day and make working on a computer more enjoyable.

Keyboards. Try the keyboard to make sure that it has a good tactile feel. Try to find one that seems to have good rugged construction. If the dealer will let you, take off the four screws on the bottom plate to see if it has a genuine hard circuit board. Some use plastic with printed circuits in conductive inks.

Other Components. You will need a printer. If you can afford it, buy a good dot matrix that is capable of printing in Near Letter Quality (NLQ). Try to get one with as many pins in the print head as possible. The less expensive ones have seven to nine pins. The better machines have 18 to 24. Try to get one that emulates the Epson or IBM extended character set. These are the characters that are used for simple graphics and foreign letters. In addition, make sure that it is capable of pixel-by-pixel graphics.

If you can afford it at all, get a hard disk drive, preferably a 20 Mb. If you can't afford about $500.00 for a 20 Mb, you might be able to pick up a 10 Mb for around $100.00.

You will probably want a modem also. There are several types. I would recommend an internal one that is built on a board. It will take up one of your 8 expansion slots, but you would have to have a serial port for an external one. An external one also takes up desk space and requires a power outlet.

There are many, many other peripherals and expansion boards that you may want later. But these items will get you up and computing.

COMPATIBILITY

When IBM introduced the PC there were several companies such as Corona, Compaq, Eagle and others, who immediately came out with compatible systems. IBM considered some of them to be a bit too compatible to be a coincidence and brought suit against several of them, accusing them of copying the IBM BIOS (Basic Input/Output System). At about the same time Apple took the Franklin company to court on the same charge and won.

Some of the companies rewrote their BIOS and continued with great success. But some did not do very well. The Franklin company lost in court and declared bankruptcy. The Eagle company was only threatened by IBM but they closed down and rewrote their BIOS. They lost several contracts while they were closed down and have never been able to recover. It's too bad, because Eagle had an excellent computer. They were the first to introduce the "Turbo" option which made their computer run almost twice as fast as the IBM's.

IBM can't be entirely blamed for Eagle's demise. It was probably my fault. I purchased 100 shares of Eagle stock when it dropped to $3.00 per share. I didn't think it could possibly go any lower. I recently sold it at ten cents a share. It seems that every time I buy a share of a company's stock, the company goes belly up the next day. IBM is lucky that I have never bought any of their stock.

Compatible Clones

In the last couple of years, several companies, most of them in the Far East, have begun manufacturing IBM compatible clones. These clones are identical to the IBM except for the BIOS. And even this is fairly close. Almost all of the 4 billion dollars worth of software that has been written for the IBM will also work on these clones. About 4 billion dollars worth of hardware has also been developed to the IBM PC standard. These clones will accept almost all of that hardware.

Compatibility Warning

Compatibility can mean different things to different vendors. To some of them it might mean that their product is compatible as far as software goes, but not hardware. For instance AT&T, Leading Edge, Tandy, and several others, have different style mother boards and configurations. Therefore you can't use any of the large number of IBM type boards that are available in these machines.

The vast majority of MS-DOS and PC-DOS software will run on the compatibles with no problem. It is possible that you might find some software that will not run on the clones. This would probably be due to the fact that the particular software was written specifically for some unique address of the IBM BIOS. If you could buy an IBM BIOS for your clone, then it would be 100 percent compatible. But IBM will only sell their BIOS to you if you have an IBM computer and the BIOS has become defective or needs to be updated. The cost would be around $40.00.

The clones have developed several BIOS versions. If you happen to find a piece of software that will not run with your BIOS, you could try one of the other versions. Most of the clone vendors can supply them for about $10.00 each.

Though it is illegal to do so, it is possible to take an IBM BIOS ROM chip from an IBM computer, place it in an EPROM burner, and make an exact copy on a blank EPROM chip. The IBM BASICA ROM chips can also be copied the same way. If these chips are then plugged into a clone, it will essentially guarantee 100% compatibility. But there really aren't that many things that are incompatible. And as we said, this is an illegal practice and we do not recommend or condone it.

Ask your vendor if their system can use the IBM type hardware, and ask if the system will run Flight Simulator and Lotus 1-2-3. If it does, then it should be fairly compatible.

THE IBM STANDARD

IBM is the unofficial standard that almost everyone is following. Apple and a few other diehards have resisted the MS-DOS or PC-DOS operating systems. Atari and Commodore now have IBM-compatible personal computers. Many companies have jumped on the bandwagon and have designed computers that are almost exact copies of the IBM. In many cases the compatibles offer more computer for a smaller price than IBM. The original IBM PC-XT mother board would accept a maximum of only 256 K of memory. For the last couple of years, many compatibles have offered mother boards that will accept 640 K. Only recently has IBM finally revised their XT mother board to accept up to 640 K of memory. The IBM PCs and clones operate at the standard clock speed of 4.77 MHz. But many of the clones can be switched to also operate at the turbo speed of 7 or 8 MHz. Many of the compatibles offer other on-board goodies not found on the IBM that we will discuss in detail later.

Most computers and computer components, just like TV's, cameras, videocassette recorders, and many other electronic devices, are now built in the Far East. It should come as no surprise that a large percentage of the components that go into the IBM computers are also manufactured in the Far East. Several companies in Japan, Taiwan, Korea and Hong Kong are now manufacturing boards, components and electronic assemblies that are identical to, and interchangeable with, the IBM PC and IBM compatible components and boards. This means that you can shop around, buy the least expensive component from one vendor, another from another vendor and still have them all fit together. If you are short of funds you can buy a bare bones basic system and add to it later.

Hundreds of small companies have begun importing these components during the last year or so. This means there is lots of competition. Many of these vendors have very low overhead. The majority of the people who run these small companies seem to be willing to accept a smaller profit margin than some other businesses. It is often a business made up of family members. They may operate out of a small store in a low rent area, or in some cases, run mail order businesses out of their bedrooms. Most of them also set up booths and sell their goods at the many computer swaps and trade shows.

There are now over six million IBM and compatible computers in use. Thousands more are being sold every day. Because of the competition and low overhead, the consumer can make some very good deals. Inflation has driven up the prices of almost everything in the world. Isn't it nice that computer prices are constantly coming down?

Chapter 2

Getting It All Together

The best reason that I can think of to assemble your own computer is that you can save over 50% of what an equivalent IBM system would cost by doing it yourself. However, you will have to shop wisely and be able to take advantage of good bargains when they arise. I have done almost all of my buying at computer shows and swap meets. There is at least one computer show or swap almost every weekend here in the San Francisco Bay Area.

COMPUTER SWAPS

Some of the swaps are much like a flea market. Many of the booths are filled with junk that looks like it was swept up off the floor, or something that was rescued from a trash can. But the shows all have a circus-like atmosphere about them and I often go just because of this.

I usually take a pencil and pad with me to the shows. I walk around and write down the prices of the items that I want to buy and compare prices at the various booths. There can be quite a wide variation in the prices. I bought my printer at a show. One dealer was asking $995.00 for it in one booth. About 50 feet away, another dealer was offering the same printer for $695.00.

You can also haggle with most of the dealers at the shows. Especially when it gets near closing time. Rather than pack up the material and lug it back to their stores, many will sell for a much lower price.

SUPPORT YOUR LOCAL STORE

I consider myself to be fairly knowledgeable about electronics and computers. I hate to admit it, but I have been burned a few times at these swaps. One reason that the components that are made in the Far East are so inexpensive is that they have not been tested very extensively. There are vendors from all over the country at some of these swaps. If you buy something from an unknown vendor, take it home and it doesn't work, you may not be able to exchange it or get it repaired.

So I would recommend that you be fairly careful at the swaps if you are not experienced. I would especially recommend that you try to find a good local vendor who could supply you with a basic barebones system that had been tested. You could then add extra components and peripherals from other sources. Then if you should buy something such as a floppy disk drive and it doesn't work, you would know that it wasn't your system that was at fault.

Again, these computers are very easy to assemble. Still, it is possible to make a mistake. And it is possible that a new part that you buy and install could be defective. Most of the dealers will give you a warranty of some kind and will replace defective parts. But if there is something in the system that prevents it from operating, you may not be able to determine just which component is defective. Besides that, it can sometimes take a considerable amount of time to remove a component like a mother board and return it to someone across town, or even worse, someone across the country.

I have dealt with Bill Boutin, the owner of Paramount Electronics in Sunnyvale, for some time. He has some fairly sophisticated test equipment and he bench tests all boards before he sells them. He says he has found solder bridges, shorts, opens, defective components and other defects on the boards that he imports. He said that it is much less expensive to test a board before it is used than to try to determine what might be wrong after the customer has put it into a case.

If at all possible, try to deal with a knowledgeable vendor who will support you and help you if you have any problems.

MAIL ORDER

Every computer magazine carries pages and pages of advertisements for these compatible components and systems. If you live in an area where there are no computer stores or shows, this would be a good way to get started. Most mail-order businesses are honest, but there are always a few who are not. Some of these dealers are rather small companies and they may no longer be in business by the time their magazine ad is published. So you might check in previous magazines to get an idea of how long they have been in business. Except for sometimes having to wait for two weeks or more for delivery, I haven't heard of any problems with mail order vendors.

BURN-IN AND INFANT MORTALITY

Unlike mechanical devices, there is nothing in a semiconductor to wear out. If an electronic circuit is designed properly, and operated within the design limits, it should last several lifetimes. But if you try to push too much power through a semiconductor, it can burn up very easily. Ordinarily, if an electronic component is going to fail, it will fail within the first few hours of operation. This is called infant mortality. If the circuit operates for at least 168 hours under full load, or at the worst condition that it will ever see, then it will probably last longer than you do.

You should turn on your new computer and let it run continuously for about a week. This is called burn-in. Some vendors do this before they offer a unit for sale. But many do not have the time or the facilities to do so.

CALL THE VENDOR

You should be sure of what you need and what you are ordering. Some of the ads aren't written very well and may not tell the whole story. If possible, call them up and make sure. Ask what their return policy is for defective merchandise. Also ask how long before the item will be shipped. And ask for the current price. The ads are usually placed about two months before the magazines are delivered or hit the stands. The way prices are coming down, there could be quite a change in cost at the time you place your order. Of course, if you send them the advertised price, I am sure that they will not refuse it. A two or three dollar phone call could save you a lot of time, trouble, grief and maybe even some money.

SOURCES OF KNOWLEDGE

There are several good magazines that can help you gain the knowledge needed to make sensible purchases and to learn more about computers. These magazines usually carry some very interesting and informative articles and reviews of software and hardware. They also have many ads for computers, components and software. We will list just a few of them. Write to them for their latest subscription prices.

1. Byte Magazine,
   70 Main St.,
   Peterborough, NH 03458

2. Computer Currents
   5720 Hollis St.,
   Emeryville, CA 94608

3. Computer Shopper,
   407 S. Washington Av.,
   Titusville, FL 32796

4. InfoWorld,
   1060 Marsh Road
   Menlo Park, CA 94025

5. MicroTimes Magazine
   5951 Canning St.,
   Oakland, CA 94609

6. PC Magazine,
   One Park Av.,
   New York, NY 10016

7. PC Week, Circulation Dept.,
   One Park Av.,
   New York, NY 10016

8. PC World Magazine
   555 De Haro St.,
   San Francisco, CA 94107

9. Personal Computing,
   10 Mulholland Dr.,
   Hasbrouck Hts., NJ 07604

Note: PC Week costs $120.00 a year for a subscription. But it is sent free to those individuals who meet their qualifications. Write to them. It is an excellent magazine.

MicroTimes and Computer Currents are also free at most computer stores in California. Microtimes currently costs $12.00 a year to have it mailed to your home. Computer Currents will be sent to you free if you meet their qualifications.

Another source of computer information can be found in the several good computer books published by the TAB Book Company.

We are not listing the names and addresses of the clone vendors and importers because there are so many of them. When I decided to build my first clone in January of 1985, I had trouble finding as many as 20 different vendors. I decided to write an article about my experiences and started to keep a file on all the vendors and importers that advertised in national and local magazines. I also attended all of the local computer shows and swaps and listed those who were there. Within six months my file had grown from 20 names and addresses to over 150. They were proliferating faster than rabbits in springtime.

If you need a source of components, you only have to look in any of the magazines listed above to find hundreds of them. If you live near a large city, there will no doubt be several who advertise in your local paper.

Chapter 3

Assembling an XT Compatible

This chapter will discuss the basics of assembling clones, and will tell you what you need to get started.

TOOLS NEEDED

We suggest that you have a pair of pliers and a couple of screwdrivers. You should have both a Phillips and a blade type screwdriver. You might even get a couple of different sizes of each because some of the screws are rather small. Though not absolutely necessary, 1/4 inch and 3/8 inch nut drivers will help speed up the assembly. But these tools are handy to have around the house even if you are not going to build a computer.

It would also help if one of the smaller Phillips and one of the blade screwdrivers were magnetized. They are very useful for picking up and holding small screws to get them started. If you can't find one that is already magnetized, you can make your own. Just take a fairly strong magnet and rub it on the shaft and end of the screwdriver a few times.

Be careful that you don't lay one of your diskettes on a magnetized screwdriver, or any other magnetized object. A magnet can erase data on a diskette and ruin it. Figure 3-1 shows the basic tools you need.

PARTS NEEDED

The parts you need are shown in Fig. 3-2. They are:

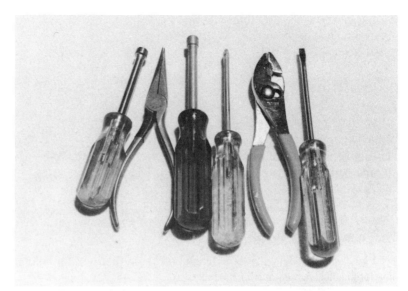

Fig. 3-1. Tools needed.

1. A case, flip top or slide on.
2. A mother board with components installed (would recommend a turbo board with 640 K of memory).
3. A power supply, 130 watt minimum.
4. A floppy disk drive controller card (or board).
5. One or two floppy disk drives.
6. A monitor card (or adaptor), should be monochrome or color, depend-

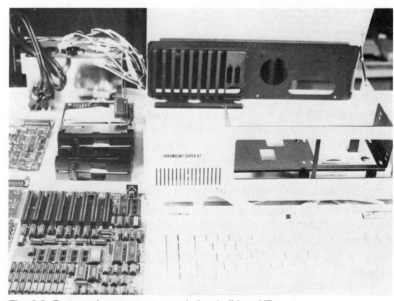

Fig. 3-2. Parts and components needed to build an XT.

ing on the type of monitor you buy.

7. A monitor.
8. A keyboard.

Optional Parts

9. A 20 Mb (megabyte) hard disk.
10. A hard disk controller card.
11. A multifunction card with clock/calendar and printer ports, both serial and parallel.
12. A printer.
13. A modem.

PRELIMINARY ASSEMBLY

The case should have a large black bracket in the front for holding the floppy disk drives and hard disks.

You should get a bag or a package of hardware with your case which would have screws, nuts, plastic guides for the front end of the boards, and rubber feet for the case.

The rubber feet may be mounted with screws, but most of them have an adhesive. Just peel off the protective tape and apply near the four corners on the bottom of the case.

Install the plastic card guides on the back of the front panel. Use silicon rubber cement or almost any kind of household cement to hold them in place.

If the back and front panels are not assembled, you should do that now.

INSTALLING THE MOTHER BOARD

The mother board (Fig. 3-3) is mounted on the bottom of the case, but it is held up about 3/4 of an inch off the floor by nine standoffs. You may have received a plastic, snap-in type of standoff, or they may be brass with threads on each end.

The standoffs should be inserted from the back of the mother board, and secured with a nut if you have the brass ones. There should be a plastic or paper insulating washer on each side of the mother board to prevent shorting out a circuit board trace.

After you have installed the standoffs, it should look like Fig. 3-4.

It is easier to plug the speaker wires into the pins on the front of the mother board before you install the mother board. It can be done later if necessary. The speaker should have a plastic holder that fits over the voice coil. Later, it will be mounted behind the front panel with two screws.

Figure 3-5 is a line drawing showing the location of the major components. There is a note in the upper right corner about the jumpers to

Fig. 3-3. A mother board with speaker attached.

select for the type of RAM memory on board. Your board may or may not have these three pins and a shorting block. There are several boards and each have slight variations. If you have 640 K on board, or the capability to install it later, then the dealer should have jumpered this correctly. If it is on your board you should check it before you install the mother board because afterwards it will be under the disk drives and be inaccessible.

You should also know at this time what kind of configuration you will have to start out. So it would be a good idea to set the DIP switches to the proper setting while they are easy to get at. The DIP switch is located about two inches in front of the 8088 CPU. A retracted ball point pen works great for setting these small switches. The following are the various settings for different configurations:

☐ 1 is normally set OFF
☐ 2 normally OFF. Set to ON for 8087

Fig. 3-4. The back side of the mother board showing the installed standoffs.

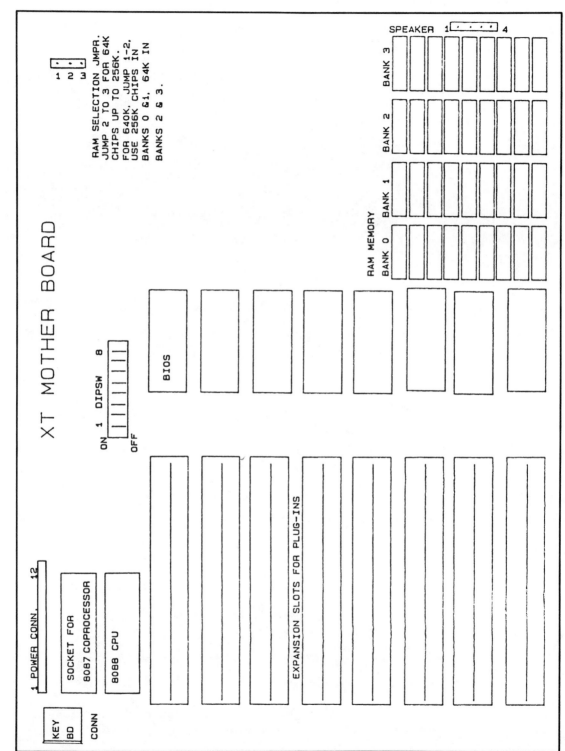

Fig. 3-5. A line drawing of the major components on the mother board.

- [ ] 3 OFF, 4 ON if only 128 K on board
- [ ] 3 OFF, 4 OFF if you have 256 K or more
- [ ] 5 ON, 6 OFF for color
- [ ] 5 OFF, 6 OFF for monochrome
- [ ] 7 ON, 8 ON if only one floppy drive
- [ ] 7 OFF, 8 ON for two floppies installed

The large black bracket for holding the disk drives should be installed already. But you will have to loosen the four screws to allow the front part of the mother board to slip under it.

Once you have the board under the disk holder, move it around a bit and the standoffs should line up and fall into the nine holes in the bottom of the case. Re-tighten the four screws for the disk holding bracket and put the nuts and washers on the nine standoffs. You may not have received washers for the bottom threads. If not you might use a bit of nail polish on the threads to keep them from becoming loose and falling off. You should be careful not to tighten the nuts too much. The brass is very soft and easy to strip.

Your unit should now look like that of Fig. 3-6.

INSTALLING THE POWER SUPPLY

The power supply is mounted in the right rear corner of the case as shown in Fig. 3-7. Four screws through the back panel hold it in place.

We are now ready to plug in the power connector to the mother board. The mother board power supply connector and the power supply are shown outside the case for clarity in Fig. 3-8.

Fig. 3-6. The case with the mother board installed.

Fig. 3-7. The power supply installed.

There are two connectors from the power supply, usually marked P8 and P9. It is possible to plug them in wrong. **It is critical that the four black wires be in the center of the connector** after both are plugged in. If they are plugged in the wrong way, you could severely damage and possibly ruin your mother board components.

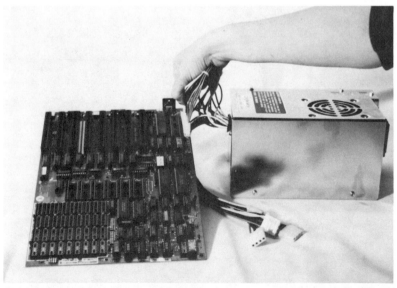

Fig. 3-8. A view outside the case showing the power connection to the mother board.

Fig. 3-9. A floppy disk drive.

INSTALLING THE DISK DRIVES

We are now ready to install our disk drives. You may have one or two drives that are similar to the one pictured in Fig. 3-9. Figure 3-10 is a side view of a couple of disk drives, showing the mounting screw holes. The holding bracket is slotted, (see Fig. 3-11) so that it is easy to slide the drives in from the front, line them up, and install the screws.

The drive or drives can be mounted in any one of four positions on the bracket. Most people prefer to mount the two floppies in the left positions, with the B drive on the bottom and the A drive on top. The hard

Fig. 3-10. A view showing the threaded holes for mounting the floppy drives.

17

Fig. 3-11. The power connected to the floppy drives.

disk drive is usually mounted in the right section, but it is entirely up to you.

Connecting Power to Disk Drives

Figure 3-12 is outside of the case for clarity. It shows the connector

Fig. 3-12. A view outside the case that shows the four cables from the power supply and one of them connected to a floppy disk.

Fig. 3-13. A 20 Mb hard disk drive.

on the back of the drive for the power. It is a four wire cable with a plastic connector that can only be plugged in one way. There are four identical cables from the power supply. They can be used to power up to two floppies and two hard disks.

Figures 3-13 and 3-14 show the top and bottom of a 20 Mb hard disk.

Fig. 3-14. The rear of the hard disk drive showing the connectors.

If you have one, it is installed in the same manner as the floppy disk drives. It uses the same type of power connector. In Fig. 3-14, the power connector is the white plastic enclosed pins on the right side.

FLOPPY DISK CONTROLLER

Figure 3-15 is a floppy disk controller. It has a 34 pin edge connector on the front of the card for a cable that can control two internally mounted floppy drives. It has a 37 pin D-type connector on the rear of the board that can accept a cable to control two external floppies. The 62 pin edge connector on the bottom of the board can be plugged into any one of the eight slots on the mother board. Most people use the number 7 or 8 slot that is nearest the drives.

Figure 3-16 shows a floppy controller with ribbon cables connected on the front of the card and also a connector from the rear connector attached to an external drive.

Your controller card may be a bit different from this one. Some of the newer ones are leaving off the external connector. I would recommend that you try to find one with the external connector if you expect to add more drives, for instance, an external 1.2 Mb floppy or a 3 1/2 inch drive. These connectors are also used by some types of tape backup systems.

Critical. Note that the ribbon cable has three identical 34 pin connectors. There is one on each end and one in the middle. It is possible to plug the connector onto the wrong edge connector, and also to plug the connector in upside down. Note that the ribbon cable to the connector on one end has been split and twisted. This connector should go to your A drive. The connector in the middle goes to the B drive if you have

Fig. 3-15. A floppy disk controller card without cables.

Fig. 3-16. A floppy disk controller card with cables attached for internal and external drive. An external floppy drive is attached.

one and the connector on the end goes to the floppy controller.

Figure 3-17 is a close up of the twist in the A drive connector. If you look closely at the connectors you will see that they have one side numbered 2 through 34, or just a 2 on one end and 34 on the other. All of the even pins are on this side. The other side has all the odd numbers and they are all ground. The odd numbers should be on the bottom of the board when connected to a disk drive. I have put a white label on mine and marked them so it is easy to see.

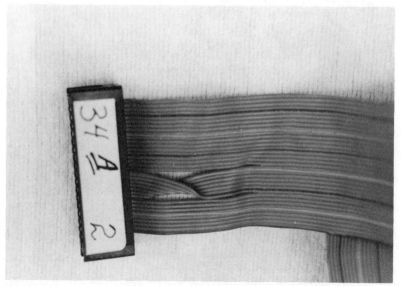

Fig. 3-17. The connector that goes to drive A will have the cable split and twisted.

ALL DRIVES INSTALLED

Figure 3-18 shows all drives installed and connected. The board nearest the drives is the floppy controller. The long board near it is the hard disk controller board. It has two ribbon cables from connectors on the front that go to the hard disk. One of them is a 34 pin connector, the other is a 20 pin. They also must be plugged in properly. Some of them are keyed so that they can only be plugged in one way. If yours isn't, look at the numbers on the connector and match it to the numbers on the circuit board.

There are several different types of hard disk controllers. Some of them are rather complicated, with several switches and jumpers so that they can be configured and used with a variety of hard disk drives. The manuals and documentation that come with most of them are very difficult to understand and follow. If at all possible, have your dealer set up your hard disk controller and configure it to your hard disk. It might be a good idea to have him format your hard disk for you also.

Figure 3-19 shows a system with a short card hard disk controller.

MONITOR AND MULTIFUNCTION CARDS

Figure 3-20 (A) shows a Paradise multifunction card. It has a clock/calendar, a serial port, 384 K of memory, a print spooler and a RAM disk.

Figure 3-20 (B) shows a Color Graphics Adapter (CGA) card to drive the monitor. It has a nine pin connector that will drive RGB type monitors, and also an RCA type jack for the less expensive composite monitors.

Fig. 3-18. A view showing boards installed and disk drives connected to a long controller board.

Fig. 3-19. A view of a different system that has a short hard disk controller board.

COMPLETED SYSTEM

Figure 3-21 shows a completed system. Before you turn it on you should check the DIP switches on the mother board for your configuration. Check all connectors to make sure they are plugged in the right way and are properly seated. Check the boards to make sure they are seated all the way down in the 62 pin slot connector. Some are a little tight and difficult to fully seat.

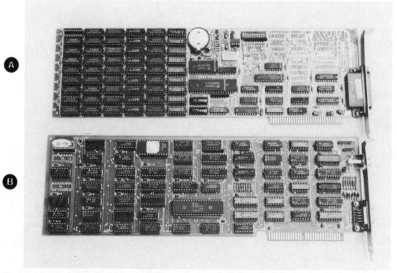

Fig. 3-20. A multifunction board (A) and a CGA board for the color monitor (B).

Fig. 3-21. Showing the completed system.

After you have done all of this, plug in your key board (Fig. 3-22) to the connector in the back, insert a copy of DOS 2.1 or 3.2, whichever you have bought, turn on the power, and start hacking.

If you have connected every thing properly and all of your components are good, then it should work great. You have a machine that is worth many times more than what you paid for it, compared to the price of an IBM. And yours will do everything the IBM can do.

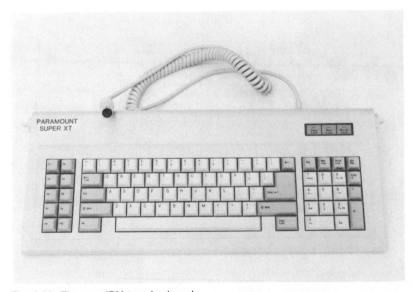

Fig. 3-22. The new IBM type keyboard.

24

Fig. 3-23. My system.

Figure 3-23 shows my XT. It has given me excellent service and I have enjoyed it very much.

If you decide to assemble a system, I would strongly recommend that you plug all the components together before you install them in the case. Turn the computer on and boot it up. It should work. If it doesn't, it is very easy then to return the parts or troubleshoot the computer. This could save you a lot of time. See Fig. 3-24.

Fig. 3-24. A system assembled outside the case and tested before installation.

Chapter 4

Assembling an
AT Compatible

The AT is very much more powerful and complex than the XT, but it is not much more difficult to assemble.

You will need the same tools for assembling an AT that you needed for an XT.

You should have a case, a cover and a bag of hardware. See Fig. 4-1. Figure 4-2 is a close up of the hardware and the case. The bag of hardware should have a speaker, plastic card guides, rubber feet, standoffs for the mother board, fillers for the unused slots on the back panel, plastic slides for the disk drives, small brackets to hold the drives in place, nuts and screws, a battery holder, and a plastic holder to mount the speaker and the front panel lock and key.

INSTALLING THE MOTHER BOARD

Installing the mother board is actually simpler on the AT than on the XT. Only two screws are used to install it. Figure 4-3 shows the AT mother board. Figure 4-4 shows the back side of the mother board with the four plastic standoffs installed. Figure 4-5 is a close up of the plastic standoffs. Two of them will be like the black one. It has a horizontal groove to receive the edge of the mother board when it is installed.

Figure 4-6 shows the two standoffs for the edge of the board. There are two standoffs in the center of the case for the only two screws that are used to hold the mother board in place.

Fig. 4-1. The case and hardware.

Component Locations

Figure 4-7 is a close up of the mother board showing the white connector for the board power supply. Figure 4-8 is a line drawing of the layout of my mother board. Yours may be different, because there are several companies who make them.

SW3 must be set for the type of monitor that you will be using. On

Fig. 4-2. Another view of the case and bag of hardware.

Fig. 4-3. The mother board.

my system, it is pushed forward for color and to the rear for monochrome. SW1 is a shorting bar that selects 6 or 8 MHz. It should almost always be set for 8 MHz. On the other side of the keyboard connector is connector J28 which is two rows of pins for a parallel port connector. You can buy a special cable, such as that pictured in Fig. 4-9, and connect this port. This will save you from having to use a board and a slot for your parallel port. There are two serial ports, COM1 and COM2 also on the board. Like the parallel port, they are just pins that stick up off the board. You will have to buy cables in order to use them. But again, they can save the cost of a board and the use of a slot. COM2 is inaccessible once the power supply is mounted, so if you intend to use this port,

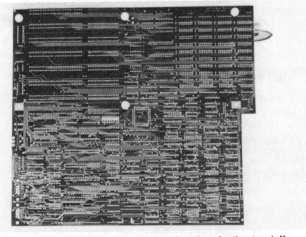

Fig. 4-4. The back side of the mother board showing the plastic standoffs.

28

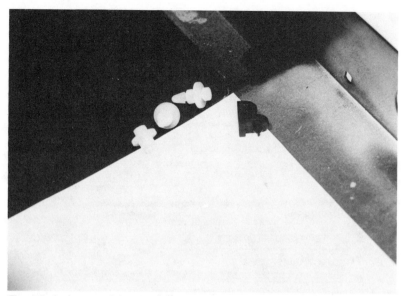

Fig. 4-5. A closeup of the standoffs.

you should buy a cable and install it before installing the power supply.

The AT normally supports two serial and two parallel ports. If you use those on the mother board, there are some pins and shorting bars at J4, J5, and J6 that should be installed or removed to enable or disable ports on the mother board. Unless the ports on the mother board are

Fig. 4-6. The floor of the case showing the standoffs and the raised metal tabs for securing the power supply.

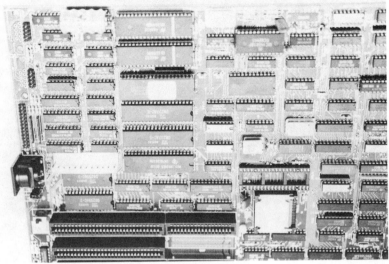

Fig. 4-7. A closeup of a portion of the mother board.

disabled, you cannot use a port from a board installed in a slot. Again, your system may be different from mine. Be sure to get some kind of documentation for your board from your dealer.

Just in front of the keyboard connector are pins to connect the battery. The AT has a portion of its boot ROM in low power CMOS semiconductors so that they are powered up at all times. My system uses 4 alkaline type AA batteries. They should last for at least two years. The battery holder is mounted to the back panel, just above the key board connector.

INSTALLING THE POWER SUPPLY

Figure 4-10 shows the bottom of a power supply showing two sections where a cut has been made and the metal pushed inward. If you look back at Fig. 4-6 again, you will see two raised metal tabs in the area where the power supply will be installed. These raised tabs slip into the cut sections on the bottom of the power supply. Two screws are then used to attach the power supply to the rear panel. The metal tabs save you from having to install about 4 screws.

Connecting Power to Mother Board

Figure 4-11 is a close up showing the connection to the power supply. This connector is the same as the connector for the XT, and it can be installed backwards. **It is critical that you install the connectors so that the four black wires are in the center.**

30

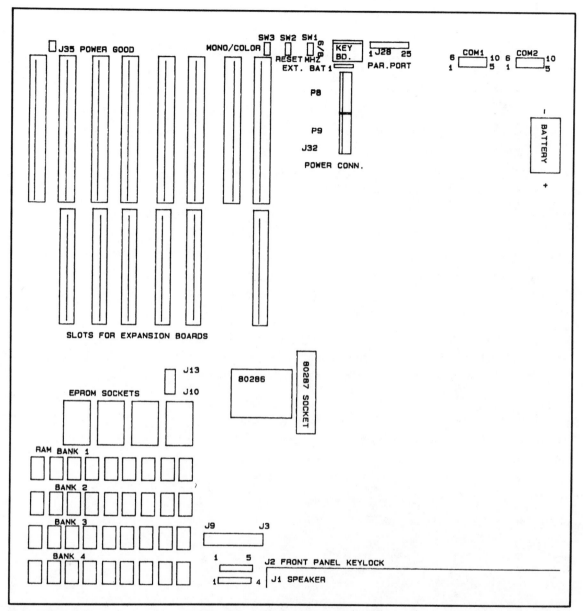

Fig. 4-8. A line drawing showing the major components on the mother board.

Power to the Drives

Figure 4-12 is shown outside the case for clarity. It shows the power connection to a disk drive. These connectors are the same as those on the XT. The power supply also has four power cables for disk drives like the XT. All four cables are identical.

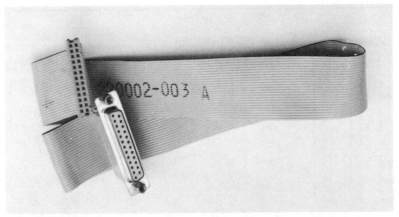

Fig. 4-9. A cable that can be used to connect to the parallel onboard port.

CONNECTING THE CONTROLLER CABLES

Figure 4-13 is again shown outside the case for clarity. It shows the ribbon cables from the controller connected to the drives. Figure 4-14 is a close up of the controller and its cables. Note two of the connectors have split and twisted ribbon cable. If you have two floppy drives, a connector with the split would be connected to the A floppy drive. The second connector on that cable would be connected to the other floppy. There are several companies who manufacture the AT controller, so yours may not look like mine, but it will work the same.

The AT uses the same floppy and hard disk drives used by the XT. It can use the same controllers, but the AT's controller can control a high density 1.2 Mb floppy, a 360 K floppy, and one or two hard disks.

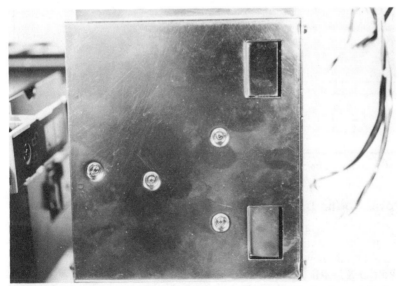

Fig. 4-10. The bottom of the power supply showing the cutouts for the metal tabs.

Fig. 4-11. The power connection to the mother board.

SPEAKER CONNECTION

Figure 4-15 shows the speaker being connected. You should have a plastic holder for it. The holder has a hole so that the voice coil can be pressed into it. The flat edge of the holder has two threaded holes for screws. The speaker is mounted to a flange on the front panel.

MOUNTING THE DISK DRIVES

If you look at the sides of the disk drives in Fig. 4-12 you will see

Fig. 4-12. How the power is connected to the disk drives.

Fig. 4-13. The disk controller cables and their connections.

that they do not have the plastic rails installed. These rails are a great improvement over XT system. Figure 4-16 shows one rail installed on the top edge of the drive and another ready to be installed on the other side.

The case is formed with grooves for the rails. They slide in easily from the front. They are then held in place by a small angle bracket with a single screw on each side. See Fig. 4-17. Whenever a disk is mounted

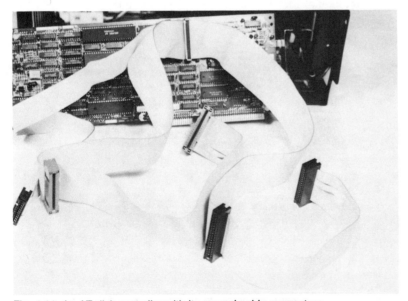

Fig. 4-14. An AT disk controller with its several cable connectors.

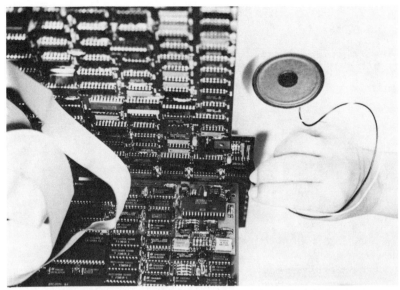

Fig. 4-15. Connecting the speaker.

alongside another, a different bracket is used on the center post to hold both drives. It is much easier to install or remove a disk from the AT than from an XT. Whenever the cover is in place and the lock is on, the brackets and case cannot be removed, so your boards and drives are fairly safe.

Fig. 4-16. Shows how the plastic rails are mounted on the disk drives.

Fig. 4-17. A close up of the brackets that hold the disks in place.

If you have a 1.2 Mb floppy and a 360 K floppy, you will mount them in the right hand slots. The left disk is reserved for hard disk and is closed when the cover is installed.

Most people mount the 1.2 Mb floppy in the upper slot and make it the A drive. The 1.2 Mb drive and the 360 K drive look very much alike except that the 1.2 Mb has an amber LED and the 360 K has a red one. You may want to label them.

Fig. 4-18. A view that shows the power connected to the disk drives.

Fig. 4-19. A side view showing one floppy disk and a 20 Mb hard disk installed with power and controller cables attached.

Figure 4-18 is a view showing the power supply connected to the mother board and to the disk drives.

FRONT PANEL KEYLOCK CONNECTION

The front panel key lock should be installed and connected. Refer

Fig. 4-20. Shows controller cables connected. Notice that the split and twisted cable is on the top drive, which makes it drive A.

Fig. 4-21. A top view showing all the cables and wires for front panel connected.

to your documentation for the connections for the green power on indicator and the red hard disk indicator.

COMPLETED

Figure 4-19 shows the controller cables connected to a single floppy drive and a 20 Mb hard disk drive. Figure 4-20 shows two floppy drives installed. Figure 4-21 is a top view of the completed system. Figure 4-22 is a front view showing my 40 Mb hard disk.

Figure 4-23 is an Enhanced Graphics Adapter (EGA) card. An EGA is necessary for high resolution monitors.

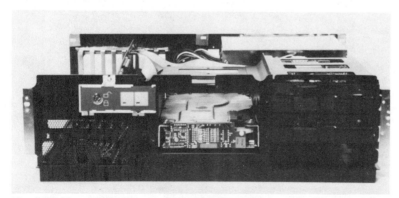

Fig. 4-22. My system with a 40 Mb hard disk system.

Fig. 4-23. A VuTek EGA card for driving a high resolution monitor.

UP AND RUNNING

Figure 4-24 shows my system up and running. I am quite pleased with it. I don't know how I ever got by with my old XT for all this time.

My system with an EGA card, a high resolution monitor and a 40 megabyte hard disk drive cost me about $2500.00. An equivalent IBM system would have cost about $6500.00 at the prices in late 1986. I'm sure the price of a clone AT will be even less by the time you read this. What a marvelous age we are living in, which offers us this technology for such a small price.

Fig. 4-24. My system up and running.

Chapter 5

How to Upgrade an Old IBM Personal Computer

There are thousands of genuine IBM computers out there that are obsolete. This includes the original PC, the PC-XT and the PC-AT. These computers may have been the latest state of the art when they were sold, but if they are more than a month old, then there are several goodies that they don't have. If they are more than a year old, they are practically antiques.

If you have one of these, you could put an ad in the paper and try to sell it, but you probably won't get much more than ten cents for each hard earned dollar that you originally spent on it. You are much better off keeping it and upgrading it.

The automobile business brings out a new model every year. Computer technology evolves much quicker. There are new models and additions announced almost daily. If you want all the latest doodads and fancy fringes on your car, you only have to buy a new car once each year, but not so in the computer business. Every IBM personal computer that has been sold since early 1981 can be easily upgraded to perform as well as the newest one off the production line, and it can be done for much less than what a new computer would cost.

ORIGINAL PC

IBM announced the original PC (for Personal Computer) on August 2, 1981. It was a historic moment. Whether you realize it or not, our way of life has been dramatically influenced and changed forever more because of this announcement and the computer that was introduced.

A lot of people criticize and take potshots at IBM, myself included. But you must give them credit for bringing some kind of standard out of the chaos that was reigning at the time. When IBM introduced the PC I, there must have been at least 100 different computer manufacturers. Each one of them had their own disk formats. Many of them had their own operating systems. Software had to be written to fit each format. But IBM with its vast resources and reputation for quality, soon forced a de facto standard.

Since most of the computers being sold were IBM, most of the software was written for IBM. Soon several other computer manufacturers began making compatibles. This increased the base for software developers even more.

Third party manufacturers began making boards and other plug-ins and improvements for the IBM PC. It had an open architecture with five slots that allowed one to configure it in many different ways for specific applications.

Evolution of the PC, XT, and AT

The original PC I, introduced in August of 1981, came standard with 16 K of RAM. It could be expanded up to 64 K maximum. Its BIOS did not support the installation of a hard disk drive. It had five slots and a 62 watt power supply. It cost over $3000.00.

The PC-XT was introduced in March of 1983. The XT was for eXtra Technology. It had eight slots and a hard disk drive. It came standard with 128 K of RAM and could accept up to 256 K on board. With 128 K, one 360 K floppy drive and a 10 Mb hard disk drive, the cost was $4,995.00.

Soon after the introduction of the PC-XT, the PC II was announced. It was very similar to the PC I, except that it now came standard with 64 K of RAM which was expandable up to 256 K. It still had the five slots, but the BIOS now supported the installation of a hard disk. But it still had the 62 watt power supply so the addition of a hard disk might have been more than the power supply could handle. The price started at about $3000.00. By the middle of 1984 the cost of the XT had dropped to about $4,300.00, and the PC II had dropped to $2,400.00.

The PC-AT was introduced in August of 1984. The AT is for Advanced Technology. It used the Intel 80286 Central Processing Unit (CPU) and was actually more powerful and more versatile than some minicomputers. With 512 K of RAM, a 20 Mb hard disk, a 1.2 Mb floppy and a 360 K floppy, the AT cost $5,795.00.

At the time of this writing, in late 1986, the PC II is down to about $2000.00. The XT is around $3000.00 and the AT has dropped to about $4900.00. The prices listed above do not include a monitor and driver card. An IBM monochrome monitor costs about $400.00 and the driver card, or Monochrome Graphics Adapter (MDA), about $185.00. The color monitor costs about $600.00 and the Color Graphics Adapter (CGA) costs about $160.00. The CGA can drive a monochrome or color monitor. IBM has also developed a high resolution monitor that costs $850.00, but in order to drive it, you have to buy an Enhanced Graphics Adapter (EGA) that costs about $1000.00.

Price Comparison

I am using an AT clone to write this. The enhanced IBM PC-AT comes with 512 K of RAM. My clone has 1 Mb. The IBM PC-AT has a 20 Mb hard disk. My clone has a very fast 40 Mb. The IBM PC-AT cost $4900, my clone cost me $1700. I added a NEC Multisync high resolution monitor and a compatible EGA for $800.00, for a total of $2500.00 for my AT clone. An equivalent AT configuration from IBM would have cost about $7000.00.

UPGRADING YOUR IBM

If you happen to have one of the IBM PCs, you can easily and inexpensively upgrade it. The clone hardware is designed from the de facto IBM standard. Almost everything that works in the clone will work in the IBM and vice versa. IBM is very large and it often takes them quite a while to institute changes. The clones have taken advantage of this and they come out with new and improved designs almost daily.

Power Supply

If you have the PC I or PC II, you probably should take out your power supply and buy a 130 watt clone power supply. Some vendors are selling them for as little as $60.00 now.

RAM Memory

Most of the clones made today have mother boards that will accept 640 K of RAM. Unless you have a very late IBM, your mother board will accept a maximum of 256 K. If you have a PC I, it will accept only 64 K. You can add a multifunction card with 384 K of memory, a clock/calendar, a serial and parallel port, a RAM disk, and Spooler for about $100.00.

Disk Drives

You can take out the full height floppy disk and replace it with two half heights, or a half height floppy and a half height 20 Mb hard disk. The half height floppy will cost less than $100.00. The 20 Mb hard disk will cost less than $400.00.

Monitors

You can buy a high resolution monitor for less than $500.00 and an EGA card to drive it for less than $300.00.

Keyboards

Your IBM keyboard is solidly built and has an excellent tactile feel to the keys, but the **Return** key is small, the same size of the other keys. The **Caps Lock** and the **Num Lock** keys do not indicate whether they are on or off. A new and improved keyboard, with LEDs for the **Caps Lock** and **Num Lock** keys, can replace the old keyboard for about $60.00. If you do a lot of typing, it will be well worth it.

Accelerator Boards

The IBM PC and XT operate at 4.77 MHz. The AT operates at 6 MHz. The clone XTs and ATs can operate up to 8 MHz. Some clone ATs are operating at 12 MHz. There are several boards and other hardware available that can make your IBM operate at a much faster speed. It is even possible to plug an accelerator board with an 80286 CPU into a PC or XT. You would then have almost all of the capability and speed of the best AT. It can cost from $200.00 up to $1000.00 to speed up your PC or XT. Even at $1000.00, it is a lot less than what an IBM PC-AT would cost.

Turbo Mother Boards

You can buy a clone turbo mother board that is switchable from 4.77 MHz to 8 MHz. Take out your IBM mother board and install the clone board. You could take the IBM BIOS and ROM from your IBM mother board and install them in the clone. You would then be assured of 100% compatibility. You could also use the RAM from your IBM mother board. You can buy a clone turbo mother board for about $100.00.

Be very careful when removing and installing chips. They are fragile, and one broken pin ruins the whole chip. Use a chip extractor/inserter. Also, be sure to ground your extractor, because even a little static can ruin your irreplaceable chips. It might also be wise to check whether there are any laws that make this switch illegal. Finally, upgrading your IBM this way will void the warranty, if it is still in affect, so you may want to check on this before you start.

Summary

If you have an older IBM PC or PC-XT, don't give it away or throw it away. You can easily upgrade it to be as good as the very latest clone very inexpensively. If you don't tell anyone, no one will ever know that your system is not 100% IBM.

Chapter 6

Mother Board and Plug-Ins

The original IBM PC II had a 63 watt power supply, one or two floppy disk drives and a mother board with five slots for plug-in boards. It came with 64 K of memory on the mother board with space to plug in up to 256 K. The IBM PC-XT was about the same as the PC except that it came with eight slots and a 130 watt power supply. The XT also came with a 10 Mb hard disk drive. Almost all of the clones that we will be discussing will be of the XT configuration.

There are still quite a lot of the original IBM PC's around. It is a very simple and comparatively inexpensive matter to upgrade them to the more versatile and powerful XT configuration.

MOTHER BOARDS

The mother board mounts on stand offs on the floor of the case. The nine stand offs may be plastic or brass. The stand offs attach to the back of the mother board which is then placed in the case so that the stand offs line up and protrude through the holes in the bottom of the case. Part of the front right corner of the mother board must be slipped under the disk drive mounting bracket. You will have to loosen the bracket to get enough room to slip the mother board under it.

The mother board is the most important part of your whole computer. There are several different kinds that are available. You should try to get the best one you can find. It should allow the installation of 640 K

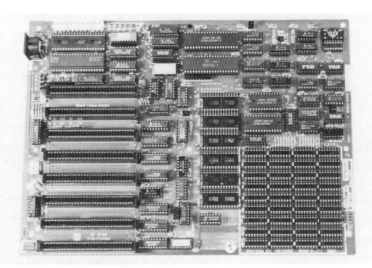

Fig. 6-1. An XT mother board.

of memory on board. It should have the capability of operating at 4.77 MHz and also at a turbo speed of 6.66 or 8 MHz. Some of the early boards were made from a single board with printed wiring circuits on each side. Most of the newer boards have four layers of printed circuits. The four layer boards are supposed to be a bit more reliable. An XT board is shown in Fig. 6-1, while Fig. 6-2 shows an AT mother board.

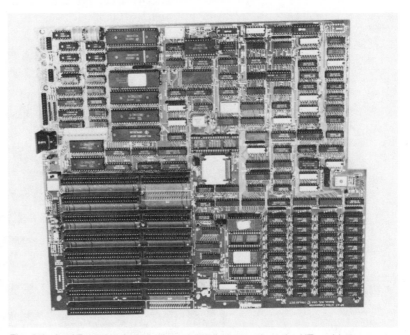

Fig. 6-2. An AT mother board. Note that it is larger than the XT and has an extra 16 bit slot connector in front of six of the eight 62 pin slots.

It is possible to buy a bare board and install the components yourself. Unless you are quite experienced, I would recommend against this. There are thousands of ways that you can make a mistake by installing a component in the wrong place or installing it improperly. Most new components will operate as they should. But there are exceptions. A very small error or defective component can prevent your computer from operating. Unless you have some very sophisticated test equipment, you may not be able to find it. Most computer repair shops charge at least $50.00 an hour. Try to find a vendor who has installed all of the basic mother board components and has thoroughly tested the assembly.

Power Supply for the Mother Board

The mother board has a connector at the right rear edge of the board for its power connection. There are two connectors from the power supply that plug into this connector. **Be sure that the black ground wires on each of these connectors are in the center.** An early XT board's power connections are shown in Fig. 6-3.

Central Processing Unit (CPU)

Alongside the power connector is the 8088 Central Processing Unit (CPU). Alongside the 8088 will be a socket where an 8087 co-processor can be plugged in. If you are going to use your computer for a lot of math and heavy number crunching, you might consider buying an 8087. They can dramatically speed up math and spread sheet operations. An 8087 will cost about $100.00.

Fig. 6-3. My early XT with an extra power connection. Note the small DIP switch that has "JAPAN" on it. These switches must be set to configure your system.

DIP Switch

In front of the CPU is a small Dual Inline Pin (DIP) switch. There are actually eight slide switches in the assembly that plugs into a 16 pin Integrated Circuit (IC) socket. These switches are set up to configure the mother board for the amount of memory, the type of monitor and the number of disk drives that will be used.

The switch will be marked ON and OFF. The circuit is configured by pushing the small tab on each individual switch to the ON or OFF side. A retracted ball point pen is ideal for moving the small tabs.

The switches are used in pairs so it is possible to have four different combinations for each two switches.

The settings shown in Table 6-1 are typical of most mother boards, but you should check the documentation for your board. These switch settings are very important. If you add another disk drive or change to a color monitor the switch settings should be changed. You might want to make a copy of them and tape it to the inside of your computer case.

Read Only Memory (ROM)

Across the middle of the mother board is a row of IC sockets for Read Only Memory (ROM) chips. The semiconductors within a ROM chip are configured and programmed for a specific purpose or task. This memory is non-volatile and cannot be written on or changed by ordinary means.

The ROM Basic Input/Output System (BIOS) chip is in the socket on the right, near the rear of the floppy disk drive. The BIOS controls the inputs and outputs from the keyboard, disk drives, modems and other peripherals. The BIOS also usually contains the boot routine that "wakes" your computer up when it is first turned on. It may check and report errors in the computer's memory and peripherals, and it generates pat-

Table 6-1. Typical Switch Settings on the Mother Board.

Switch Settings		Functions
1 = Off	2 = Off	With 8087 coprocessor
1 = Off	2 = On	Without 8087
3 = Off	4 = On	128 K of RAM memory on monitor board
3 = On	4 = Off	192 K of RAM
3 = Off	4 = Off	256 K of RAM
5 = On	6 = On	No monitor board installed
5 = Off	6 = On	Color graphics board (40 × 20 mode)
5 = On	6 = Off	Color graphics board (80 × 25 mode)
5 = Off	6 = Off	Monochrome monitor board
7 = On	8 = On	1 floppy disk drive installed
7 = Off	8 = On	2 floppy disk drives installed
7 = On	8 = Off	3 floppy disk drives installed
7 = Off	8 = Off	4 floppy disk drives installed

terns for the American Standard Code for Information Interchange (AS-CII), date and time of day, and the print screen utility.

In the four sockets immediately to the left of the BIOS in a genuine IBM PC will be the BASICA ROM. IBM PC's use the BASICA ROM for running BASIC programs. These sockets in most of the clones will be empty. But that doesn't mean that you can't run BASIC programs on your clone. You may run almost all BASIC programs on your clone if you have a disk based copy of GW-BASIC from Microsoft.

Random Access Memory (RAM)

The RAM section is located on the front left portion of the mother board. There are four rows of sockets for plugging in the RAM ICs. There are nine sockets per row or bank. It actually takes nine 8 K chips to make 64 K and nine 32 K chips to make 256 K. The ninth chip in each bank is used for parity checking and other housekeeping chores. On the standard mother board, there are four rows or banks, with nine sockets in each bank for the memory chips. To get 640 K on the board, two of the rows of sockets are set up so that they will accept 256 K chips. This would give a total of 512 K. The other two banks are filled with the standard 64 K chips for 128 K. When added to the 512 K this gives a total of 640 K.

Turbo Speed Switch

On the back edge of the board, near the left hand corner, is a small can that contains the crystal. This crystal operates at 14.31 MHz which is divided down by three to equal the 4.77 MHz operating frequency. Many of the clones have installed a second crystal that operates at 20 MHz or 24 MHz, which is then divided by three to get 6.666 MHz or 8 MHz. Some programs, especially some of the games, will not run very well at the higher speed, so the turbo systems will let you switch to the slower frequency when necessary.

OPEN ARCHITECTURE

One of the better things about the IBM PC and compatibles is the open architecture of the PC, PC-XT and PC-AT with the eight slots or plug-in connectors. You can have a bare bones system with only the absolute necessities, or you can choose from hundreds of different boards, drives and peripherals and configure your system in almost any way that you want to. Almost all of the boards, disk drives, peripherals and other goodies are interchangeable with IBM and the compatible units. But the IBM boards and components will cost you two or three times more than the equivalent clone boards. This is somewhat like owning a Ford and being able to buy and use all of the parts that make up a Cadillac at Ford prices.

Eight slots on the mother board sounds like a lot. But they can fill

up in a hurry. You would need one for the monitor, one for flop
drive controller, one for a serial port for a printer or modem, one ɪor a
parallel port for a parallel printer, one for a hard disk drive controller,
and one for extended memory, and possibly one for an internal modem
on a board. Two of the eight slots are behind the floppy disk drive area,
so only short, or half size boards can be used there.

EXTENSION BOARD FOR SLOTS

It is not often that you will be using all eight of the installed boards
at the same time. So you could take the case off and install some other
board that you might need for a special purpose. But this is a lot of trouble so IBM came up with an extension board that has an additional eight
slots and a power supply. The board is housed in the same kind of case
that the computer is in. It connects to the computer by a cable.

You could buy a complete clone computer for what IBM charges for
this extension. Or you could buy a bare clone mother board for less than
$100.00 and a case for about $50.00 and make your own extension.

SHORT BOARDS

At one time the short slots presented a problem because there
weren't too many boards available that could fit in that area. Some newly
developed chips and technological advances now allow a tremendous
amount of components to be mounted on a short slot board. Many boards
are now being built with multiple functions. AST first came out with a
long SIX-PAK board that had six functions which included up to 384 K
of memory, a parallel port, a serial port, a print spooler, a ram disk and
a clock. If the 384 K is added to the 256 K on the mother board it brings
the total memory up to 640 K, which is the maximum for the PC and
PC-XT. The AST SIX-PAK cost over $600.00 when it first came out.
Some of the Far East clone makers are now making similar boards for
about $100.00. Some of the new boards now have as many as 12 func-
tions on a single board. Many of the newer boards have several functions on a short board. Figure 6-4 shows both a hard disk controller and
a floppy disk controller.

OTHER ON-BOARD GOODIES

Some of the clones also built clocks, ports, floppy controllers and
other functions onto their mother boards so that even more slots were
freed.

BUILD GRADUALLY

As we pointed out before, another good feature about systems like
this is that you can buy a little at a time. If you can't hide enough of the
grocery money from your spouse or housemates to buy a complete sys-

Fig. 6-4. An XT hard disk controller and a floppy disk controller.

tem at one time, you can do it gradually. You can buy whatever you can afford, then wait for bargains and buy the rest when it is most convenient. Depending on how you configurate it, a system may cost from $500.00 upwards to several thousand dollars.

As we mentioned earlier, if you are a true hacker, you will never have a completed system. Hardware designers and software developers lay awake nights dreaming up new items that will do things much easier, better, and that will save you several milliseconds of time over your old methods. You will of course want to add these items to your system as soon as you can afford them.

Chapter 7

Keyboards and Other Inputs

The IBM keyboard for the PC and PC-XT is a solidly built piece of hardware, and it has an excellent tactile feel to the keys, but it has received a lot of criticism. When you press the **Caps Lock** on the keyboard, there is no indication on the keyboard to let you know whether you are in upper or lower case until you try it. The same is true for the **Num Lock** key. There have also been complaints about the small **Return** key. Several keyboard manufacturers quickly noticed this oversight and designed keyboards with larger **Return** keys and small LEDs that light up when the **Caps** or **Num Lock** keys are pressed.

KEYTRONICS KEYBOARD STANDARD

The Keytronics Company of Spokane, Washington was one of the first to come out with an alternate keyboard for the PC and the XT. They also offered an improved keyboard for the PC-AT. Their keyboards are also solidly built and of high quality.

Clone Keyboards

The clone makers recognized the excellence of the Keytronics keyboards and quickly designed imitations of them. They even went so far as to give them the same model numbers, KB 5150 and KB 5151, as those used by Keytronics.

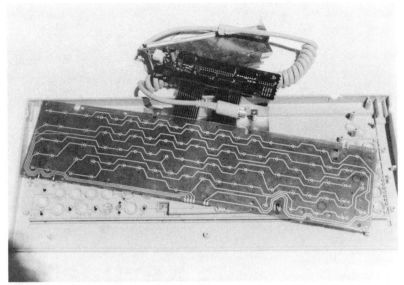

Fig. 7-1. The insides of my wine-and-coffee-ruined keyboard. It had a flexible plastic printed circuit board and used rubber cups under the keys instead of springs.

The IBM keyboards use a calibrated spring beneath the keys. Some of the clone makers use a soft rubber cup. Instead of a hard printed circuit board, some use a flexible piece of plastic. The circuits are printed onto the plastic with a conductive silver paint. Carbon dots about 1/4 inch in diameter are placed on the back side of the plastic sheet at the junction of the individual circuits for each key. The sheet is then folded over and located so that a carbon dot is located on each half of the folded sheet directly opposite each other. Each carbon dot corresponds with the location of a key. When a key is depressed it pushes down on the rubber cup which causes the two carbon dots on each half of the plastic sheet to make contact and complete the circuit. See Fig. 7-1.

Keyboard Quality and Tactile Feel

My first clone keyboard had a very soft touch. If I just barely rested my fingers on the home keys, they would take off and send all kinds of crazy things to the computer. So I took it down to a local computer swap and sold it. I would have liked to have bought an IBM or Keytronics. But the IBM keyboard would have cost about $250.00. The Keytronics costs about the same. So I bought a clone at the computer swap for $55.00. It had the rubber cups but had a tactile feel that was very close to that of an original IBM.

I used my keyboard daily for over a year with no problems whatsoever. But then one night I worked late on an article. I decided to quit and have my usual glass of wine before I went to bed. I drank about half of my wine, then decided that I should add one more sentence to the article. I sat my wine glass down near the keyboard and you can guess what happened. I found out firsthand that a keyboard cannot handle liquor very well.

I took the keyboard apart and cleaned it up. It worked fine for another six months until I sat a cup of coffee down near my keyboard one day. I found out that keyboards can't handle coffee very well either. This time I was not able to clean it up. I was rather glad that I hadn't bought a $250.00 keyboard.

So I went down and bought another keyboard. See Fig. 7-2, I paid $69.00 for it. It is built much better than the first two that I had. It has a genuine circuit board in it and the keys have calibrated springs beneath them. See Fig. 7-3. It has a good tactile feel and appears to be close to the IBM as far as quality goes. I am rather pleased with it in that respect.

I then laid down a hard and fast rule for myself that no coffee or wine was to ever come closer than three feet to my keyboard. But as you know, most rules are broken from time to time. I can do without the wine, especially when I am working. But it is almost impossible for me to work without coffee. So I set up a small coffee table to my right and beneath my computer desk. See Fig. 7-4. So far I have managed to avoid kicking the table over and spilling the coffee on the floor.

New Design

My new keyboard has a different key layout than my previous one. IBM has recently re-designed their keyboards. Of course the clones were on the street with an identical one almost before IBM had completed their press announcement.

Frankly, I am not too happy with the new layout. I don't type that

Fig. 7-2. My new keyboard.

Fig. 7-3. My new keyboard is much better quality and has a real printed circuit board and springs under the keys.

well in the first place. It took me several years to learn the old keyboard and now I have to re-learn several new key positions.

The new IBM style keyboards incorporate LEDs to indicate whether the **Caps Lock**, the **Num Lock** and the **Scroll Lock** are on or off. They also added a larger **Return** key. But they moved the **Esc** key, the **Prtsc** key, and a couple other utility keys around. I still use the older IBMs at work and it is a bit confusing at times. I have to stop and remember where I am. The older keyboards will eventually be phased out and we will learn to live with the new one.

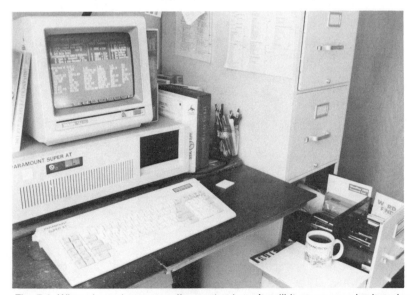

Fig. 7-4. Where I now keep my coffee so that I won't spill it on my new keyboard.

How a Keyboard Works

The keyboard has a microprocessor inside it and is actually a small computer in itself. Each time a key is pressed a unique signal is sent to the BIOS. This signal is made up of binary zeros and ones, or rather a direct current voltage that is turned on and off a certain number of times within a definite time frame.

Each time a 5 volt line is turned on for a certain amount of time, it represents a 1, when it is off for a certain amount of time it represents a 0. In the ASCII code, if A is pressed, the binary code for 65 will be generated, 1 0 0 0 0 0 1.

Special Keys

The main part of the keyboard is very similar to a typewriter layout. But there are some extra keys that we will briefly describe.

The keyboard has 84 keys, but it is possible to press two or more special keys at the same time for some functions. Keys like the **Shift**, **Control**, **Number Lock**, **Alternate** and function keys, in conjunction with other keys, can give us a very large number of virtual keys.

Function Keys. On most keyboards the function keys are the ten keys located to the left of the standard keys. They will be marked **F1** through **F10**. They are already used by most of the larger software programs. I am using WordStar to type this. WordStar has an installation menu that allows one to easily program the function keys any way they want to. I have set mine up as follows, **F1** to quit editing and save to disk, **F2** to reform a paragraph after I have changed or added something, **F3** sets the left margin to wherever the cursor is, **F4** sets the right margin to the cursor, **F5** marks a word or group of words for underlining, **F6** moves a marked block of text to a new location, **F7** marks the beginning of a block to be moved, **F8** marks the end of the block, **F9** sends the cursor to the beginning of the file, **F10** takes you to the end of the file

Some keyboards may have the function keys located across the top of the keyboard.

Numbers. There are two sets of numbers on the keyboard. The row across the top is very similar to the keys on a standard typewriter. They also have the standard symbols that are available when the shift and a number key is pressed.

The second set of numbers are arranged in a configuration similar to that of a calculator keypad. This makes it very easy to input large amounts of numeric data. The numbers on this set of keys are active only when the **Num Lock** is on.

When the **Num Lock** is off, these keys move the cursor about the screen. Then these keys are called the arrow or cursor keys.

Arrow Keys. The down arrow on the 2 key moves the cursor down one line. The up arrow on the 8 key moves it up one line. The left arrow on the 4 moves the cursor to the left, the right arrow on the 6 moves it to the right.

Home and End Keys. The **Home** on the 7 key moves the cursor to the upper left hand corner of the screen. The **End** on the 1 moves it to the bottom of the screen or end of the text. On some programs such as BASIC, pressing **Ctrl + Home** clears all information from the screen and sends the cursor to the top left corner. **Ctrl + End** will erase a line from the cursor to the end of the line.

Pg Dn and Pg Up (Page Down and Page Up). The **Pg Dn** on the 3 causes the next page to be displayed on the screen. The **Pg Up** causes the computer to page backwards through the file.

Ins (Insert). The **Ins** on the 0 key allows text to be inserted without writing over the present text. The text will continue to move to the right to allow text to be entered as long as **Ins** is on. It works like a toggle switch, turning on or off each time it is pressed. With the **Ins** off, anything typed will replace any characters at the cursor.

Del (Delete). The Del on the period or decimal key will delete the character at the cursor. All characters to the right will move to the left to fill in the gap.

Esc (Escape). Most programs utilize this key in some way, to leave a program, to erase a line, or many other functions.

PrtSc (Print Screen). By pressing the **Shift** key and the **PrtSc** key, anything on the screen will be sent to the printer and printed out. The asterisk on this key has different meanings depending on the program or mode that you are in. For most calculating programs, it means times or multiplication. For instance, 4*15 would mean 4 times 15. In DOS, the * can be used as a "wild card" for copying or manipulating files. For instance, if you had several files that had the extension .BAK and you wanted to erase all of them, you could give the single command, ERASE *.BAK.

Scroll Lock/Break Key. The **Scroll Lock** has different functions in different programs. When the **Ctrl** key is pressed along with the Scroll Lock/Break key, the computer will usually interrupt what it is doing and take you back to where you were. For instance, say I don't have my printer hooked up to my computer at this moment. I press the **Shift** and **PrtSc** key and everything hangs up. The computer was trying to print out the contents of the screen but couldn't because the printer was not there. The only way I could regain control would be to press the **Control** and **Scroll Lock/Break** key.

Backspace. The backspace key is a left pointing arrow at the top right on the standard numeral key row. It moves the cursor backwards one character at a time. In some programs, it erases the character to the left of it as it moves backward.

Return or Enter Key. This key is used to tell the computer that you have finished that particular line or entry. You can type several hundred lines, but if you do not press the Enter key, it will not be sent to the computer's memory. In most word processors, the Return or Enter key is used only at the end of a paragraph. When the cursor reaches the end of your right margin, most word processors automatically wrap around and send the cursor to the left for the next line.

Shift. There are two shift keys that operate in the same manner as those on a typewriter. They are used to print the upper case capital and the standard symbols on the numeric keys.

Caps Lock. This key is similar to the shift lock key on a typewriter, except that it affects the letters of the alphabet only. If you want to type in a $ sign for instance, you must use the **Shift** key whether or not the **Caps Lock** is on. When the **Caps Lock** is on you can also use the shift keys to type a lower case letter of the alphabet.

Ctrl (Control). The **Control** key is used in conjunction with several other keys for a variety of purposes. If you ask to view a long directory with the DIR command, it may scroll up the screen very quickly. You can use the **Ctrl** and **S** to stop it, then press any key to start it again. **Ctrl** plus **C** will abort the directory and return you to the prompt sign of what ever disk or file you were in.

Tab. The Tab key has a left and a right pointing arrow with a bar at the end of each arrow tip. The **Tab** key ordinarily works just like the tab key on a typewriter. However, it will move the cursor backwards to tab stops when the **Shift** key is used with it. Not all programs allow the use of the backward tabs.

Alt (Alternate). The **Alternate** key can have a variety of functions depending on the particular software program. It is most often used with **Ctrl** and **Del** to re-boot or re-set the computer system. Sometimes the computer will hang up. For instance you may give the computer a command to perform a certain task. It will drop everything and try to do it. If part of the program is missing or for some reason the task cannot be performed, the computer may continue to try, ignoring any requests from you to come back. Often there is no way out except to use the **Ctrl** + **Alt** + **Del** to re-set the system. This clears the memory and anything that has not been saved to disk will be erased. There are times when even this warm boot will not clear the computer. In such cases you will have to turn off the power and turn it back on again.

REPROGRAMMING KEY FUNCTIONS

The keys can be changed by various software programs to represent almost anything you want them to. One thing that makes learning computers difficult is that every software program uses the special keys in a different way. You may learn all the special keys that WordStar uses. But if you want to use a word processor such as Multimate, Peachtext or any of the others, you will have to learn the special commands and keys that they use.

MACROS

There are several keyboard programs such as SUPERKEY, PROKEY and others that will allow you to program one or more keys to represent a whole word, a sentence or even a whole file. For instance you could have a program that would type out your name and address when the **Alt** key and the A key were pressed together. If your work entails a lot of repetitive keystrokes, the macros can save you a lot of time.

PC-AT VS PC-XT KEYBOARDS

The PC-AT and the PC-XT keyboards may look exactly alike and have the same type of connector. But their internal frequency rates are different, so you cannot use an AT on a XT or vice versa. I bought my XT and AT keyboards from the same vendor. There were no markings on the outside of them and to me they looked exactly the same. I asked the technician who sold them to me if he hadn't made a mistake. He said, "Oh no. If you look closely you will see that the XT has a white cable and the AT has a black one."

Some of the clones have installed a switch beneath their keyboards that will allow them to be used on either the AT or XT.

OTHER METHODS OF INPUT

The keyboard is the most common method of accessing the computer, but it is not the only way. Here is a brief look at some of the other methods.

Mouse

A mouse is a small object that can be used to move and control the cursor. It usually plugs into a serial port on the back of the computer and works only under the control of special software programs.

There are many software programs such as graphics and Computer Aided Design (CAD) programs that are almost impossible to use without the mouse. Even programs like word processors and spreadsheets can be made easier and can be done faster with the aid of a mouse.

Most of the mice sold today use a small light on the underside of the mouse. When the mouse is moved over a reflective grid, the light is reflected each time a grid line is crossed. This is counted and input to the computer. The grid is supposed to represent the area of the monitor. But they are usually much smaller than the 13 inch monitor face. So if you start at one edge and move all the way across the grid and still can't get the cursor to where you want it, you can pick the mouse up and move it back and continue. When you pick the mouse up, the cursor remains where it was left. Since it is counting only lines you can pick it up and move it as many times as necessary. Other mice have a small ball built into their bottoms.

The mouse will have two or three buttons on top. They may perform various functions under control of the specific program you might be using. For instance, one button might be used to start the movement of the cursor, and the other might have to be pressed to end and position it.

A mouse may cost from $75.00 to over $200.00.

Trackballs

Honeywell Disc Instruments has developed a trackball that plugs in-line with your keyboard input. The keyboard is unplugged, the μLynx is plugged in, then the keyboard is plugged into the μLynx-straightthrough plug. See Fig. 7-5.

This trackball takes considerably less desk space than the mouse and the grid that it needs. And it doesn't require a wall socket power source, as some mice do.

It can be used with several types of programs, graphics, spreadsheets, and word processors.

A trackball can make using the computer much easier for the inexperienced. It can considerably increase the productivity of anyone using a computer.

At the time of this writing, the μLynx would only operate on the PC or XT. It does not work on the AT because the AT has a different keyboard. But they are working on a new model that should be available by the time you read this. Cost at the present time is $139.00.
Manufactured by:
Honeywell Disc Instruments Subsidiary
102 East Baker St.
Costa Mesa, CA 92626

Fig. 7-5. A trackball cursor controller. Can be used with many programs to rapidly move the cursor. This is similar to a mouse, but has better resolution than most mice.

Joysticks

Many of the arcade type games use joysticks to control the cursor or wipe out alien figures.

Touchscreen

The touch screen system uses a series of horizontal and vertical infrared lights around the border of the screen. These invisible lights form a grid. If a finger or some other object interrupts the light at a particular grid, the computer detects it. Then, depending on the software, the computer could move the cursor, delete a word, or many other functions.

Voice Recognition

With a microphone, special hardware, and special software, the computer can recognize spoken words and perform accordingly. This technology might be used in an area where data must be collected, but the person might not be able to use his hands to write or type it in. For instance it might be an inspector or research scientist looking through a microscope and describing an object. The person could speak directly into the microphone and input the data without taking his eyes off the object.

This technology is also used by some of our military pilots. Most of our modern fighter planes are highly computerized. The pilot is usually so busy that he hasn't the time or freedom to type in commands. Voice commands are a fast and easy way of accessing the computer.

This technology is also used on voice controlled robots and other voice actuated devices.

You can't just walk up to a computer that is equipped with voice recognition and start giving it commands. It must first be trained to recognize your voice.

As you know, not everyone speaks the same way. Some may slur certain words or run them together. They may speak very fast or very slow and they may not pronounce the words like most other people do.

The computer will be given a number of words in its vocabulary depending on what it will be used for. Since each word requires quite a lot of memory and storage, the early voice programs were limited to about 100 words or so. But since memory has become less expensive, some programs today may have 1500 and more words in their vocabulary.

To train the computer to recognize ones voice, they must speak each word of the vocabulary into a microphone. In many of the programs, the computer will display a word, then the operator will speak that word. The microphone converts the sound waves of the spoken word into voltages, which are then converted into digital ones and zeros, and then stored on disk in a file with that person's name or identity.

It really doesn't matter how a person pronounces a word. If the computer displayed the word "about" and a person from Canada pronounced it as "aboot", the computer wouldn't care. Every time it heard "aboot" from that person, it would go search that person's file and come up with the word "about". Any pronunciation, or even a foreign language can be used.

As you can imagine there are still some limitations to voice entry, but many advances have been made. Some day we will probably have voice actuated typewriters, or computers that will print out the spoken word. We will never be able to completely eliminate the keyboard, but voice will take over many of its functions. This will make the computer much more friendly and helpful to many people. Especially to those who might be handicapped or those who do not type very well.

Barcodes

For several years the grocery industry searched for better ways to keep track of the thousands of products on their shelves. In 1973 they adopted the Universal Product Code (UPC). This code is a series of vertical marks arranged to represent the numbers 0 through 9. This code is somewhat similar to the Morse code, but instead of dits and dots, this code uses narrow bars and wide bars.

Almost every manufactured product now sold in a grocery store has been registered and given a unique number that may have ten or more numerals. This number will be printed on the product and immediately above it will be the barcode that represents the numerals. The store can enter this unique number into their computer, then enter the item's price, size, quantity in stock, the vendor, and any other pertinent information that they want.

When someone buys that item, it is passed over a barcode reader. The reader emits a beep and sends the number to the computer and cash register. The computer searches for the number and the information associated with it, and causes the cash register to print out a receipt. The computer also deducts that one item from inventory and adds the cash from the sale to the sum of the proceeds of the day.

The grocer can then use the computer to determine just how much of each item he has in the store. He knows what items are selling and when he should order more. If he wants to put an item on sale, he can easily change the price of any item in the store on the computer.

The barcode system is faster and much more accurate than a human for entering the prices of items on a cash register. It is an excellent labor saving tool.

For several years the military searched for better ways to keep track of the thousands of items in the military stores. Millions of dollars were spent to have people do nothing else but take continuous inventories.

A committee looked at the success of the UPC barcode system and in 1982 they adopted a similar version. The military version is quite a bit more comprehensive than the UPC. It has 43 symbols which includes all of the upper case letters of the alphabet, the numerals 0 to 9 and most of the other symbols found on a typewriter keyboard. See Fig. 7-6.

Each bar or space is called an element. An element can be a wide bar, a narrow bar, a wide space or a narrow space. It takes 9 elements to make a character, and 3 of those elements must be wide. So this system has been called code 39, or 3 of 9. This system was developed by the Intermec Corporation.

Using this system, the letter A would have a wide black bar, a narrow space, a narrow bar, a narrow space, a wide space, a narrow bar, a narrow space and a wide bar. There are two wide bars and one wide space that make up the 3 wide elements. The rest of the elements are narrow bars and spaces. See Fig. 7-7.

There are two main types of barcode readers, the laser and LED types. Both of them detect the code by the reflected light that is swept across the bars and spaces. The black bars will absorb the light, the white spaces will reflect it. These reflections are then converted into zeros and ones and will appear to the computer just as if they had been typed from the keyboard.

Several small hand held computers have been developed for reading and storing barcode data in a storeroom or on the factory floor. Many bar readers are attached in series with the keyboard of a computer and

CHAR.	PATTERN	BARS	SPACES	CHAR.	PATTERN	BARS	SPACES
1		10001	0100	M		11000	0001
2		01001	0100	N		00101	0001
3		11000	0100	O		10100	0001
4		00101	0100	P		01100	0001
5		10100	0100	Q		00011	0001
6		01100	0100	R		10010	0001
7		00011	0100	S		01010	0001
8		10010	0100	T		00110	0001
9		01010	0100	U		10001	1000
0		00110	0100	V		01001	1000
A		10001	0010	W		11000	1000
B		01001	0010	X		00101	1000
C		11000	0010	Y		10100	1000
D		00101	0010	Z		01100	1000
E		10100	0010	-		00011	1000
F		01100	0010	•		10010	1000
G		00011	0010	SPACE		01010	1000
H		10010	0010	*		00110	1000
I		01010	0010	$		00000	1110
J		00110	0010	/		00000	1101
K		10001	0001	+		00000	1011
L		01001	0001	%		00000	0111

Fig. 7-6. The barcode 39 code. This code was developed originally by Intermec Corporation. It has since been adopted by the Military. (Courtesy Intermec Corp.)

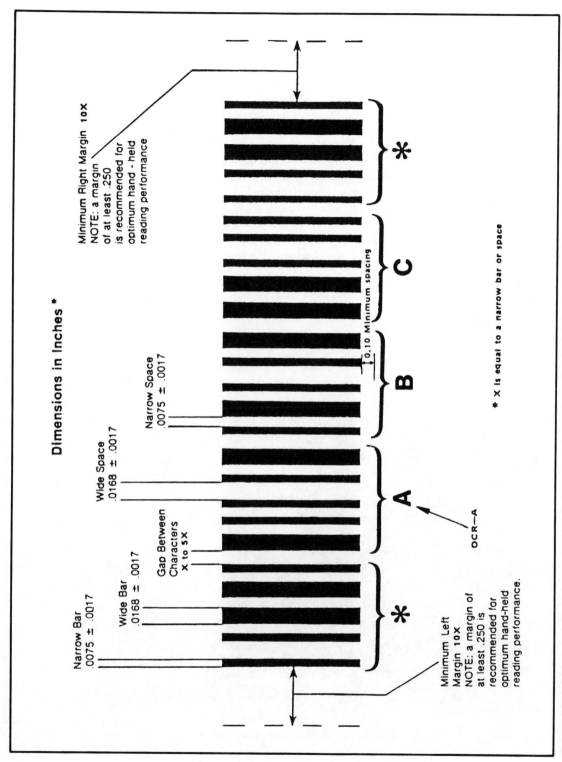

Fig. 7-7. The letters A B C in barcode with the asterisk which is the start/stop symbol much like a period.

data can be entered from either into the computer. See Figs. 7-8 and 7-9.

The military decreed that every item that they purchase should have a barcode label on the outer package, and in most cases, on the item itself. Many of the contractors screamed and moaned at the prospect of having to buy label printers and readers. But it wasn't long before they found hundreds of ways that the barcode systems could save them money, time and labor. The military saves millions of dollars in inventory costs every year.

Several other barcode systems have been developed for specialized purposes. The Blood Bank has developed their own system so that every pint of blood can be traced back to the person, place, and time where it was donated. Other systems have been developed for use in hospitals, libraries, small businesses and hundreds of other applications.

If you want to learn more about barcodes there is a barcode magazine that is sent free to qualified subscribers. To find out if you qualify for a free subscription, write to:

BarCode News
174 Concord St.,
Peterborough, NH 03458.

Optical Character Readers

Most large offices have literally tons of paper in the form of manuals,

Fig. 7-8. Barcode data accumulation instruments. (Courtesy Welch Allyn Co.)

Fig. 7-9. A plug in card that allows a computer to read and store barcode information. Entering barcode data with the wand through this plug-in would appear to the computer just like data entered from a keyboard. (Photo Courtesy Welch Allyn Co.)

memos, letters and all sorts of official records and documents that must be retained or filed and updated constantly. An enormous amount of labor is spent in organizing, filing and retrieving records and files. The bulging filing cabinets take up valuable floor space that could be better used for other purposes.

With the widespread use of computers, many people hoped that we would enter into a new era, the era of the paperless society. But almost every computer has a printer tied to it. Instead of eliminating paper, the computer has made even more paper. One of the officials of Xerox Corporation was recently quoted as saying "We will have a paperless society about the same time that we have a paperless bathroom".

In the early 1980's several companies introduced Optical Character Readers (OCR). They were rather large and expensive and not very reliable in their limited ability to read various text fonts and text arrangements.

In the last few years the OCRs have been improved and enhanced. They are smaller and more compact, but more versatile in their ability to read and scan various types of text and fonts. The prices of the OCR's are also much more reasonable. See Fig. 7-10.

Pages of text are fed into the OCRs and a camera scans the lines and detects the dark and white areas of the paper. The camera digitizes this information into white and black pixels with a resolution of about

Fig. 7-10. An optical scanner that can read printed material, convert it to digital information and send it to computer. Once in the computer it can be edited with a word processor or stored on disk. Instructions and manuals take much less space on a disk. Files can be easily searched for, updated, deleted or transmitted to another computer. (Photo courtesy of DEST Corporation.)

300 X 300 per inch. It has sample font types and text stored in its memory. The machine compares the scanned text with its stored memory. When a character is recognized it is sent to a computer.

To the computer, characters sent from an OCR are no different from those received from a keyboard. A whole page of typewritten text can be read and sent to a computer in about 25 seconds. Once it is in the computer, it can be stored on a floppy or a hard disk. Of course, once it is in the computer, it can be easily called up, edited, revised or updated as necessary.

There are many advantages of having documents and records in a computer. A floppy diskette can store 30 to 40 pages of documents. A 10 Mb hard disk could store several volumes. The documents can be stored in files so that an individual record can be searched for and found almost instantly. If necessary, a hard copy of the record could be printed out or transmitted by modem to another computer on the other side of the country.

The OCR scanners cost from $2000.00 up to $10,000.00 depending on the model and the accessories that are ordered. Not too many people could justify buying one of these for their personal use at home. But in a large office, a computer and one of those desktop machines can pay for itself many times over by eliminating many of the filing cabinets and the costly labor of of filing and re-filing.

Chapter 8

Power Supplies

You know that you have to have power to the computer in order for it to operate. If you don't know a little bit about electronics, you may not be aware of what happens after you plug it into the wall socket.

The voltage that comes out of the wall socket is 110 volts ac, or alternating current, but the various integrated circuits and components in the computer require dc, or direct current, voltages of +5 volts, −5 volts, +12 volts and −12 volts. It is the function of the power supply to convert the 110 volts ac into the required dc voltages.

WHERE IT PLUGS IN

The power supply is that covered box that sits in the right rear corner of the computer. It will have four separate cables with connectors for disk drives. They can be plugged into two floppy drives and two hard disk drives or any combination. They each have four leads whose functions are shown in Table 8-1.

There are two other cables, usually marked P8 and P9 that plug into the mother board. They plug into the connector that is parallel to the 8087 socket near the edge of the board. The pin numbers and functions are shown in Table 8-2.

The PC-AT power supply leads have the same colors and functions. The only difference between the XT and AT power supplies is that the

Table 8-1. Power Supply Connections to the Disk Drives.

Pin #	Color	Function
1	Yellow	+ 12 vdc
2	Black	Ground
3	Black	Ground
4	Red	+ 5 vdc

XT supply is usually 130 to 150 watts, while the AT supply will be 190 to 200 watts.

HOW POWER SUPPLIES WORK

Up until a few years ago, most power supplies required a line transformer. The greater the power that had to be supplied, the larger and heavier the line power transformer.

A transformer is made by winding layers of insulated wire on a special iron core for the primary, then winding other layers of wire on top of this for the secondary. When the primary winding is attached to the 110 volts ac, the alternating current causes a magnetic flux to increase and then decrease in the iron core each time the current alternates between positive and negative. This swinging magnetic flux causes an alternating voltage to be induced into the secondary winding of the transformer.

The amount of voltage induced into the secondary winding will be determined by the ratio of the number of turns of the primary to the secondary. For instance, if we have 100 turns on the primary and 10 on the secondary, and 100 volts is input to the primary, then 10 volts will appear on the secondary windings.

If we wanted a higher voltage on the secondary than on the primary, say for instance 1000 volts, then we could wind 1000 turns on the secon-

Table 8-2. Power Supply Connections to the Mother Board.

Pin #	Color	Function
P8-1	White	Power good
P8-2	—————	No connection
P8-3	Yellow	+ 12 vdc
P8-4	Brown	− 12 vdc
P8-5	Black	Ground
P8-6	Black	Ground
P9-1	Black	Ground
P9-2	Black	Ground
P9-3	Blue	− 5 vdc
P9-4	Red	+ 5 vdc
P9-5	Red	+ 5 vdc
P9-6	Red	+ 5 vdc

dary over the 100 turns of the primary. With that transformer, we could apply 10 volts to the primary and get 100 volts on the secondary.

Wattage

Getting 100 volts out of 10 volts looks like we are getting a lot more power out than what we are putting in. But we aren't. Power, or wattage, is calculated by the amount of voltage times the amount of current, or amperes. If we input 10 volts at 10 amps that would be 10 v × 10 a = 100 watts. If we boost the 10 volts at 10 amps up to 100 volts, we will still have only 100 watts because our current would drop to 1 amp.

Power supplies have to be designed to handle the maximum amount of wattage that will be drawn from them. If you try to draw more current than what the supply was designed for, the transformer and other components will get hot and may burn up or short out.

Line Frequency

One of the factors that affects the amount of wattage or power that can be passed through a transformer is the frequency of the alternations. For some reason, in the early days of our electrical system, 60 cycles per second, or 60 Hertz, was chosen. We would be a lot better off had they chosen a higher frequency. Electric motors, appliances and many electronic items could be much smaller and more efficient. A motor that is designed to operate at 400 Hz can be about one fourth the size of one that would yield the same horsepower at 60 Hz.

Over the last few years, high voltage power transistors have been developed. This has made it possible to change the frequency of the input voltage to our power supplies.

The first thing that is done to increase the line frequency is to make direct current out of the 110 volt ac line voltage. This is done by passing it through rectifiers or diodes. The dc voltage is then chopped up at a frequency of 20,000 to 50,000 cycles or Hertz (Hz) by high voltage power transistors. This high frequency voltage is then passed through a small transformer to bring it down to the required low voltages. These low voltages are again rectified and turned back into the dc voltages our computer circuits need.

With this high frequency, an entire 150 watt switching power supply weighs less than the transformer alone would weigh in a 60 Hz system. Figure 8-1 shows the components inside a switching power supply.

Regulated Voltages

Some of our computer circuits are rather finicky, and they require a very stable, or regulated, voltage. If you put a heavy load on an unregulated supply line, the voltage will drop. If you have a couple of boards in your system and they are using 5 volts at 2 amps, then you add two more boards, to draw 4 amps, the voltage will drop way down. Again,

Fig. 8-1. Inside a switching power supply.

remember that we are talking about power, or wattage, which is voltage times current.

A regulated supply is designed so that it can supply the extra current at the same voltage if the load is increased or decreased. It is similar to a cruise control on an automobile. You can set the speed you want and it will remain fairly constant going uphill or downhill because the cruise control feeds the engine more or less gasoline as necessary to maintain a constant speed.

Fans

Ordinarily, there should be no sound when you switch on your computer. Those little electrons are very quiet when they go speeding around inside the silicon chips.

The sounds you hear are from the cooling fan in the power supply and the motors of the disk drives. The fan is needed primarily to cool the power transistors in the supply.

WHAT SIZE POWER SUPPLY DO YOU NEED?

The original IBM PC had a 63 watt power supply. This was adequate to supply the power needed for one or two floppy disk drives. It could also supply as many as five boards, the limit that could be plugged into the PC. But it wasn't long before people started adding hard disk drives and types of boards that drew more current. So there were instances when the 63 watt supply just wasn't big enough.

The clone makers recognized this fact and they flooded the market with larger supplies at very reasonable prices. A 130 to 150 watt supply will usually be adequate for the PC-XT and compatibles. The PC-AT requires 190 to 220 watts when fully loaded with accessories.

Plugging into the Power Line

When you finally get all of your system, you will probably have five or six line cords to be plugged in. This could include your computer, your monitor, your printer, your modem and maybe a mouse. Most of these items will have a three wire power plug so that they can only be plugged in one way. But most of the older houses still have the two wire power outlets. Most people will either cut off the "u" shaped ground pin so that they can use the two wire outlets, or they will buy an adapter.

The two wire outlets should have one fairly wide slot which should be ground or neutral. The narrower slot should be hot. But some of the older homes may not be wired properly. I would recommend that you use a voltmeter to check out the wiring. If you don't have a voltmeter, most hardware stores have small neon lamp voltage indicators that can determine which of the two wires in the outlet is hot.

If you should plug in a piece of equipment with high voltage on the ground pin of the unit, and plug in another piece in the opposite way, you could possibly have 110 volts on the chassis of a unit. If all of the equipment is not plugged in properly to the same side of the line, you could have a lot of grounding problems. I would strongly recommend that you buy a power strip that has at least six three wire outlets such as that shown in Fig. 8-2. Then buy an adapter and make sure that the power strip is plugged into your two wire outlet properly. A six outlet strip can be purchased for $10.00 to $15.00.

SURGE SUPPRESSION

When your refrigerator turns on, or when any other heavy inductive

Fig. 8-2. A recommended power outlet strip.

load is placed on the line, the voltage can drop, and high voltage spikes can be fed back into the line. These spikes could cause some problems if they are not filtered out. Most of the outlet strips boast that they have surge protection. But it usually consists of a ten cent ceramic capacitor that is wired from the hot side to ground.

There are professional controllers that may have from two to four outlets. These controllers have electronic filters and suppressors. They may cost from $70.00 up to $200.00. I am not sure that they are actually needed. Maybe I have just been lucky, but I have gotten by for several years without one.

POWER INTERRUPTIONS

Usually when you are working on a computer, data and whatever you are doing to it, is stored in RAM (Random Access Memory). If the power is interrupted, even for a brief second, all of the data in memory is lost.

I work in an office with a lot of other people. There are several electric coffee pots and hot air popcorn poppers in the area. A couple of times, I have had two or three hours of work disappear because someone would turn on all the coffee pots and popcorn machines at the same time. This would cause a circuit breaker to trip and all of my data to vanish. I learned the hard way that I should save my work to disk every ten or fifteen minutes. Then if the power should go off for any reason, I would still have most of my work on disk.

I have a small den at home where I have all of my computer equipment. I have a six outlet power strip for all of my equipment and this strip is plugged into a single wall outlet.

I brought my two year old granddaughter over one weekend but I wasn't able to pay too much attention to her because I had a deadline to meet for an article that I was working on.

I had worked on the article for about three hours and almost had it finished. I was so intent on getting it finished that I did not notice my granddaughter wander in. She went straight to the wall outlet and unplugged my computer. She is only two years old, but I swear she did it on purpose because I was ignoring her. I should have been saving the data to disk every ten or fifteen minutes.

Winter storms and lightning can also cause power interruptions. If at all possible, save your work to disk often.

POWER BACKUP

There are backup power supplies that can take over in the event of a power outage and provide emergency power for up to a half hour. These units have a rechargeable battery that is constantly charged up by the line voltage. In the event of a power outage, a power transistor circuit takes over, chops up the dc voltage from the battery and supplies 120 volts of alternating current to the computer. Depending on the number of outlets required and the amount of wattage, the backups may cost from $400.00 up to $700.00.

I am not sure that the kind of work that I do would justify buying one, but if your applications are critical, $700.00 might seem like a small amount to spend in order to make sure your data is secure. We almost never have any electrical storms on the west coast. If you live in an area where there are lots of power outages it might be worthwhile to invest in a power supply backup.

ONBOARD BATTERY BACKUP

Some of the newer CMOS integrated circuits draw very small amounts of power. Some of the clock circuits that are available today are powered by a lithium battery that can last up to ten years.

Most of the present memory circuit ICs still require a fairly large amount of power. But the technology is advancing every day. It is probable that in the very near future, there will be CMOS type memory circuits that can be backed up with an onboard battery.

Chapter 9

Drives, Disks and Diskettes

This chapter covers floppy disks, hard disks, and tape backup systems.

HOW FLOPPY DISK DRIVES OPERATE

The floppy drive spins a diskette much like a record player. The floppy diskette is made from a type of plastic that is coated with an iron oxide material. It is very similar to the tape that is used in cassette tape recorders. The disk drive uses a head that records (writes) or plays back (reads) the diskette much like the record/playback head in a cassette recorder. When the head writes on the iron oxide surface, a pulse of electricity causes the head to magnetize that portion of track beneath the head. A spot on the track that is magnetized can represent a 1. If the next spot of the same track is not magnetized, it can represent a 0. When the tracks are read, the head detects whether each portion of the track is magnetized or not and outputs a series of 1s and 0s accordingly.

Rotation Speed

It is obvious that the speed of the disk drive and the length of time that a pulse is applied will be a factor in the amount of data that can be recorded. Most of the 5 1/4 inch floppy drives rotate at 300 rpm. The AT high density 1.2 Mb rotates at 360 rpm and the 3 1/2 inch drives may operate at up to 600 rpm. Hard disks rotate at 3600 rpm. The speed is critical and should be regulated fairly close.

Number of Tracks per Inch

Another factor that determines the amount of data that can be placed on a diskette is the format and number of tracks. If you look at the head slot on each side of the diskette, you will see that there is only a little over one inch of usable space on a 5 1/4 inch diskette. The IBM PC and XT record at 40 tracks per inch (TPI). The newer 1.2 Mb disk drive has 96 TPI.

THE IBM STANDARD FORMAT

The IBM system uses a Double Sided Double Density (DS/DD) format that allows 360 K bytes to be recorded on a diskette.

Before a diskette can be used it must be formatted. As we said earlier, at one time each manufacturer had his own format. But now most of them are standardizing on the IBM system. This system calls for the diskette to be formatted with 40 tracks, each track being divided into 9 sectors. See Fig. 9-1.

If you took the outer square covering off the floppy diskette, it would appear to be similar to one of the old 45 rpm records. Like a record player, the diskette spins and has tracks. But a record has a single groove that winds from the outer edge to the center. A diskette has separate individual tracks and each of the tracks is divided into sectors. A maximum of 512 bytes can be recorded on a track within one of these sectors.

Fig. 9-1. A floppy diskette that has been taken apart. Lines representing tracks and sectors have been drawn on the diskette.

Heads

Many of the early disk drives had only a single head and recorded on one side of the diskette only. Most all of the drives today have two heads, one for each side of the floppy diskette. Both heads are controlled by a single positioner. If track 1 is being read on the top side, the bottom head is over track 1 on the bottom side. The positioner moves the heads to whatever track or sector needs to be written to or read from.

Clusters

Since 512 bytes is rather small, DOS treats two sectors on a track as a single unit and calls it a *cluster*. For instance, if you have a file that has 3 K bytes, the computer might place 1024 bytes in sectors 0 and 1 of track 1. If the next cluster, sectors 2 and 3 of track 1, already has data on it, the computer will send the next 1024 bytes to the first available open cluster which might be on track 20. The directory of the diskette has a File Allocation Table or FAT that keeps track of where each part of the file was placed. This system allows you to add onto an existing file by placing the addition in any empty cluster. You may delete any part of a file by erasing one or more clusters.

No two files with different names, or parts of two different files, can reside in a single cluster. A cluster is made up of two sectors, each having 512 bytes, for a total of 1024 bytes or 1 K. (Notice that 1 K, or 1 kilobyte, which one would expect to be 1000 bytes, is actually 1024 bytes. This anomaly of computer science comes about because of the computer's preoccupation with binary numbers. 1024 is simpler to represent in binary, because $2^{10} = 1024$.) It doesn't matter if a file has only one byte or 1024 bytes in it, it will require one whole cluster of 1024 bytes. If a file has between 1025 bytes and 2048 bytes, it will require two clusters.

Most hard disk formats are similar to the floppy format, except that the hard disks usually have many more tracks, may have 17 or more sectors per track and may use four or more sectors to form one cluster.

The Number of Bytes on a Floppy Disk

Each side of the disk has 40 tracks, each consisting of 9 sectors. This means that each side of the disk has $40 \times 9 = 360$ sectors. Since each sector can store 512 bytes, that gives us $512 \times 360 = 184320$ bytes on each side of the disk. A two sided floppy disk therefore has the capacity for 368640 bytes, or 360 K. (Again, note that 1 K is actually 1024 bytes.) If you run CHKDSK (checkdisk), however, it will tell you that you only have 362496 bytes on the disk. The other 6144 bytes are used by the FAT to keep track of what and where everything is on the disk.

Maximum Number of Files Per Diskette

As we pointd out above, each side of a floppy has 360 sectors. This means that we have 180 clusters on each side of the diskette. Each cluster could be a separate file, therefore we could possibly have 360 files on one diskette. But the FAT, the directory and other overhead files, require a certain amount of the space, so the maximum number of files that you can put on a single 360 K diskette is 112. The maximum number for the 1.2 Mb is just twice that, 224.

To prove this to myself, I took a newly formated diskette and used WordStar to make 120 files. Each file consisted only of a name which was a number from 1 to 120. Though there was nothing in the files, Word-Star reserved 128 bytes for each file. I recorded all of these files on my hard disk, then tried to transfer them to the floppy in drive A. When it tried to record file number 113, I got a message that said "File Creation Error." A CHKDSK showed that there was 247808 bytes of free space on the diskette but there was no way it could be used unless more data was recorded in the existing files.

FLOPPY CONTROLLERS

The PC and PC-XT floppy controllers can control up to 4 drives. The floppy controllers have a connector on the front of the card for two internal drives. There is a 37 pin connector on the back of the card that is accessible from the rear of the computer. Two external drives can be connected to this connector. Some tape backup systems use this connector to back up the hard disk, but the external connector on the back of the floppy controller is not used on most computers. Many of the less expensive controllers leave this connector off so that only two disk drives can be controlled.

ATTACHING CONTROLLER CABLES TO DISK DRIVES

Each of the floppy disk drives have a 34 pin edge card connector for connection to the controller card. A flat 34 wire ribbon cable provides this connection. This cable has a connector on each end and one in the middle. The cable has one red wire on one edge that indicates pin one. A couple of the wires that go to the connector on one end have been split and crossed over. This connector goes to floppy disk A. The connector in the middle goes to floppy disk B. It might be possible to plug the ribbon cable in backwards, but most of the connectors are keyed. If they do not have a key, then look at the connector. There will usually be numbers by pins 2 and 34 and there are usually matching numbers on the drive board.

If you have two disk drives, you might want the top one to be the A drive and the bottom to be B. Just plug the connector with the twist into the drive on top to do so.

THE VIRTUAL DRIVE

The person who has but a single floppy drive also has a second floppy drive, because of a slick trick by the computer. Since the computer can use only one floppy at a time, it can regard drive A as also being drive B. If you want to make a backup copy of an important diskette, you can put the diskette in A, at the A> type DISKCOPY A: B:. The information will be read off the diskette into memory, then the computer will ask you to remove the original and place the target diskette in drive B:. The computer will move the information out of memory and onto the diskette. Having an actual second floppy drive merely saves you the trouble of switching disks. So if you are just getting started, you can get by fairly well with a single floppy disk drive. The advantages of having a second floppy are very slight. It would be much better to save the money and buy a good hard disk drive to go with the floppy.

Remember that you must set the DIP switch on the mother board to reflect the number of drives that you have installed. For one disk drive, both 7 and 8 should be on. (See page 15.)

TYPES OF FLOPPY DRIVES

IBM used the full height drive in their early PC. The half height soon became available and was used on most other computers. But IBM stayed with the full heights until the AT was developed. I am not convinced that the full height is that much more reliable than the half heights. I have an IBM PC-XT on my desk at work. It is a little over a year old. The disk drive has had to be repaired twice. If it had been up to me I would have thrown the drive away and bought a new one. Most computer repair shops charge from $50.00 up to $100.00 an hour. I have seen floppy disk drives for as little as $50.00 apiece.

3.5 Inch Floppy

There are other types of floppy drives. At one time IBM was pushing for a 4 inch type drive but not many companies accepted it. Sony introduced a 3.5 inch drive and this type system has been adopted by several companies. They are light and are ideal for portables. See Fig. 9-2 for a comparison of their sizes.

The new IBM laptop computer uses 3 1/2 inch floppies which have 80 tracks per side and can be formatted to store 720 K bytes. There is little doubt that it will be the standard for 3 1/2 inch floppies.

The 5 1/4 inch floppies are housed in a fairly thin square envelope. It is quite possible to bend the floppy, or damage it in some way. There is also an opening for the head on each side so that the diskette can be touched or contaminated with dirt and other deleterious materials.

The 3 1/2 inch floppies are housed in a hard cover and it has a seal that covers the head opening when it is not in use. The 3 1/2 inch diskettes are small enough to fit nicely in a shirt pocket, and they will not be damaged if you do this.

Disk technology continues to advance at a fantastic pace. Some floppy formats between 1.8 and 2.5 inches have been developed for use in some of the new electronic still cameras.

Fig. 9-2. A 5 1/4. inch floppy and a 3 1/2 inch side by side.

Quad Density

There are some 5 1/4 inch systems that read and write 80 tracks per side. These are called quad density. 720 K bytes can be stored on each of these diskettes. These drives, which double the amount that can be stored on a diskette, can be installed in the IBM PC-XT. They require a special controller and software to install one of these drives on an IBM or compatible system.

1.2 Mb Drive for PC-AT

The IBM PC-AT uses a 1.2 Mb floppy disk system. This system uses a more expensive diskette with a fine grain high coercivity type of iron oxide. This means that its 96 tracks per inch can be magnetized to a greater extent than the standard diskettes.

This high density drive can read the single sided 160 K and 180 K, or the double sided 320 K and 360 K format diskettes, but it cannot write in the other formats. If you try to erase a file, or write on one of the lower format diskettes, it may damage data on the diskette.

There have been several reports that the 1.2 Mb is not very reliable in reading the lower density diskettes. I have encountered the problem several times myself. It works great on 1.2 Mb disks, but not on the lower density disks. I have been told that this is a problem not only with the clone ATs, but also with the genuine IBM drives.

1.2 Mb Drive for the PC and XT

Weltec Digital of Anaheim has recently developed a disk drive for

PCs and XTs that will record at the 1.2 Mb high density used on the AT. This drive connects to the standard floppy controller. It is supplied with on-board electronics and software that make it compatible with the PC or XT controller. The drive or drives can be mounted internally or externally. When mounted externally, it is plugged into the 37 pin connector on the end of the controller card. One of the plugs from the power supply must also be brought out for the drive motor power. See Fig. 9-3.

This drive would be an ideal way for those people who have invested in a PC or XT and would like to improve their systems. If your boss is too cheap to buy one for the computer you use at work, you could buy an external one for your computer at home, then take it to the office and plug it into the IBM or compatible on your desk. At the end of the day, unplug it and bring your work back home on the disk and continue working at home. They weigh about three pounds and easily fit in a briefcase. This would be much better than lugging a portable back and forth. Of course, if you had a 1.2 Mb drive at work and one at home, you would only have to carry the diskettes back and forth. The drives cost about the same as the AT type drives, less than $150.00 each.

HIGH DENSITY DRIVES

Several drives are now available which combine the high storage capacity of hard disks with the portability of floppies. They are expensive, but for certain applications they can be quite ideal.

3.3, 6.6 and 12 Mb Drives

Kodak, the film people, are now in the computer business. They have

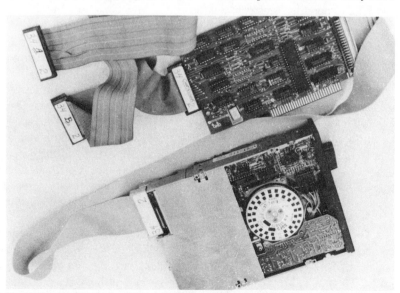

Fig. 9-3. A Weltec Corporation 1.2 Mb floppy disk drive that can be used on an XT. Shown connected to the external connector of the floppy controller.

developed disk drives that can format floppies to 3.3 Mb and 6.6 Mb. The drives use a very high density 5 1/4 inch diskette that looks very much like a standard diskette. The drives are competitively priced, the 3.3 is $285.00 and the 6.6 is $390.00. These drives also have the capability of reading the 1.2 Mb and 360 K formats. Kodak also has a 12 Mb 5 1/4 inch removable cartridge diskette. This drive lists at $970.00 each.

The Bernoulli Box

The IOMEGA Company has a high density floppy that can store 10 Mb on a removable cartridge. On most floppy systems the head directly contacts the diskette. The heads on the IOMEGA system "fly" microinches above the diskette, like the heads on a hard disk. Anyone who has ever taken a physics course is familiar with Bernoulli's principle of aerodynamics. This principle explains how an airplane can fly.

The IOMEGA company applied the Bernoulli principle to the heads in their drives, thus the name. The Bernoulli Box is a good system, but it costs from $2000.00 up to $4000.00, which is rather expensive when compared to other alternatives.

Advantages

The high density diskettes and removable cartridges have several advantages over hard disks. You always have to worry about a hard disk crashing, or being erased accidentally. There is also a problem of data security if the computer is in a business area. Several people use the computer on my desk at work. It would be very difficult to use it to store any kind of data that was confidential. But a high capacity floppy, or a cartridge, can be removed and locked up in a secure area.

High density disks also make the data more transportable. A program can be developed on one computer, then the diskette or cartridge can be moved to another computer to continue working.

Many software programs such as dBASE III and Lotus 1-2-3 are copy protected. If they are installed on a hard disk of a computer, they can be used only on that computer. It isn't often that a person will be using all of the programs on a hard disk in one session. If a person is using that computer to do something like word processing, none of the other programs on the hard disk can be used by anyone else. So if you had three or four computers in an office area you would need to buy several copies of the protected programs and install one on each computer, and yet these expensive programs could be idle much of the time.

This could cost a considerable amount of money. Unless all of your computers were using the same copy protected program at the same time, it would be less expensive to install high density drives on each computer. Then install the copy protected programs on high density floppies and use those programs only on one computer at a time, as needed.

DISK DRIVE POWER

Both floppy and hard disk drives have identical four pin connectors that supply power to the motors. The power supplies have four separate cables that can be plugged into two floppies and two hard disks or any other combination.

CARE OF DISKETTES

The heads actually contact the diskette, so there is some wear each time a disk is read from or written to. They can be used several hundred times before they wear out, but you should make backups of your master diskettes and of any others that have important data.

Each diskette has a write protect notch. If this notch is covered the diskette can be read, but it cannot be written on or erased. All of your masters and important data diskettes should have this notch covered. It is very easy to hit the wrong key and write over or erase a very important or expensive diskette.

It is very important that the diskettes be kept clean of dirt and foreign substances. You should be careful not to touch the diskette through the open slot which is the head contact area. Oils from fingerprints can destroy data. You should also be careful not to allow any magnetic objects near your diskettes.

I recently brought home some floppy diskettes, with important data on them, from Chicago. I didn't want to take a chance of having them damaged in my regular baggage, so I put them in a carry-on bag which was passed through an X-Ray machine. When I got home and tried to run the programs, the diskettes were blank. The X-Ray machine had completely erased them. Luckily, I was able to get a replacement through the mail.

PRICE OF DISKETTES

The price of diskettes can vary greatly. The 96 tracks per inch (TPI) 1.2 Mb high coercivity type diskette for the PC-AT may sell for as little as $1.70 each for generic brands and up to $10.00 each for name brands. The brand name standard double sided double density (DS/DD) diskettes may sell from $2.50 up to $5.00 apiece, but there are several non-brand name companies who sell the generic type for as low as forty cents apiece. I have bought hundreds of the low cost diskettes and have found very few that had bad sectors. When the diskette is formatted, if any sectors are found to be bad, it is marked by the File Application Table and is not used. A diskette could have 20 K or more of bad sectors and you could still use it. When I do find one with bad sectors I use it for a work or scratch diskette.

HARD DISKS AND MASS STORAGE

One of the first hard disk drives that IBM developed had a large 30

Mb hard disk that could be removed, and a 30 Mb fixed internal hard disk.

An interesting story explains why hard disks came to be called Winchester drives. The Winchester House of Mystery, a tourist attraction, is located in San Jose, not far from IBM. This house was built by the widow of the famous inventor of the Winchester .30-.30 rifle.Since the IBM hard disk was a 30/30 system, someone hung the name Winchester on it. It stuck and all hard disks that use that original technology are known as Winchesters.

Technically, IBM refers to the Winchester as a Direct Access Storage Device, abbreviated DASD. It is pronounced as DAZ-dee.

You may not feel that you need a hard disk system. You would only feel this way if you have never used one. There is an intoxicating feeling of power in knowing that you have several hundred programs at your fingertips that can pop up on your screen within milliseconds.

Many of us computer users are like pack rats. We glom onto every piece of software that we can get hold of and store it for possible future use. You could store them all on floppy diskettes, but if you are not very well organized, and you have a couple hundred floppies, it may be difficult to find what you need. This is one of the best reasons to have them all on a hard disk. Of course, you still need to keep the floppies just in case something happens to your hard disk.

In many cases you may not ever have a need for a lot of the software that you accumulate. But there is some kind of immutable and inflexible law that decrees that if you throw something away, you will almost certainly need it the next day.

It is a well known fact of life that you can never have too much money, too much memory, or too much disk storage.

If a person is constantly downloading software from the Bulletin Boards, or exchanging programs among friends or in users groups, or buying all the latest issues, it won't take long to fill up a 10 Mb hard disk and lots of floppies.

Vendors are practically giving away 10 Mb hard disks nowadays. A few months ago a 10 Mb system cost from $1500.00 to $2000.00. Most magazine ads offer 10 Mb systems for under $300.00, and I have seen some for less than $100.00 today.

I would recommend that you install at least a 20 Mb hard disk system. You can now get a 20 Mb system with a controller card for less than $400.00.

HOW A HARD DISK OPERATES

The original hard disks were 12 to 14 inches in diameter and up to 1/4 inch in thickness. They required large, massive drives, and cabinets full of electronics. Most of the drives sold today are about the same size as the half height 5 1/4 inch floppy drives. It is possible to get as much as 40 Mb or more in one of these half height drives. It is possible to get 30 Mb or more in a 3 1/2 inch hard disk drive.

The hard disks use a format that is similar to the one used on floppies, but one of the differences is that the hard disk has tracks that are closer together. A floppy disk may have from 40 to 96 tracks per inch but a hard disk may have 600 to 1200 TPI.

Another major difference is the speed of rotation. A floppy disk rotates at about 300 rpm. A hard disk rotates at 3600 rpm. Reading and writing magnetic media depends on the rate at which individual bits can be read or written. At the higher speed, the frequency of the magnetizing pulses can be much higher and the duration can be much shorter.

The amount of magnetism that is induced on a diskette when it is recorded is very small. It must be small so that it will not affect other tracks on each side of it, or affect the tracks on the other side of the thin diskette. A head detects lines of magnetic flux. Magnetic lines of flux decrease as you move away from a magnet by the square of the distance. So it is desirable to have the heads make contact with the diskette.

As we said earlier, the floppy disk heads actually contact the diskette. This causes some wear, but not very much because the rotation is fairly slow and the plastic diskettes have a special lubricant and are fairly slippery. But heads of the hard disk systems never touch the disk. The fragile heads and the disk would be severely damaged if they made contact at the fast speed of 3600 rpm. The heads "fly" over the spinning disk, just microinches above it. The air must be filtered and pure because the smallest speck of dust or dirt can cause the head to "crash." Figure 9-4 shows what can happen to a disk when a head crashes.

Fig. 9-4. Why you need to back up your hard disks often. The disk on the left has hoplessly crashed with no chance recovering any data at all. Some data can be recovered from less serious crashes. The disk on the right is shown for comparison. (Disks were photographed with courtesy of Rotating Memory Service of Santa Clara.)

The surface of the hard disk platters must be very smooth. The heads are only a few millionths of an inch away from the surface so any unevenness could cause a head crash. The platters are usually made from aluminum and lapped to a mirror finish. They are then coated with a magnetic material.

The platters must also be very rigid so that the close distance between the head and the platter surface is maintained. You should avoid any sudden movement of the computer or any jarring while the disk is spinning. IBM put out a diagnostic disk for the XT that has a SHIPDISK command. This command can be used to park the heads in a safe area of the disks any time that the computer is to be moved or shipped. Most of the newer hard disk systems automatically move the heads away from the read/write surface when the power is turned off. If you use this command on a non-IBM hard disk, it may just cause the system to hang-up and force you to re-boot.

Multiple Disks

So that more recording surfaces can be crammed into a 5 1/4 inch disk hardware format, a hard disk system may have from two disks up to as many as 10 or more. All the platters are stacked on a single shaft with just enough spacing between each one for the heads. Each disk has a head for the top surface and one for the bottom. If the system has four disks, then it will have eight heads. All heads are controlled by the same positioner and they will all move as one. If head number one is over track one, sector one, then all the other heads will be over track one, sector one on each disk surface.

Cyclinders

A cyclinder is all of the tracks that would be under the heads at any one time. If there are eight heads and they are all positioned over track number one, then all eight of the circular tracks are considered to be cyclinder number one. If you could strip off all the other tracks and material on either side of track number one, then stacked the tracks one on top of the other, it would resemble a cyclinder. Even the tracks on each side of a floppy are considered to be a cyclinder.

A system can perform faster by using cyclinders. Depending on the type of disk, it takes a finite amount of time to move a head from one track to another. The positioner must find the track. The heads move fairly fast and may overshoot the track a bit, so there is a settling time that is necessary for the head to be perfectly positioned. If a hard disk is spinning at 3600 rpm and the eight heads are over track number one, it is a lot faster to record as much data as possible on track one, side zero, then track one, side one, and then track one of all the other platters before moving to another track. All eight track ones could be recorded without having to use the time to move the heads.

Head Positioners

There are several different types of head positioners. Some use stepper motors to move the heads in discrete steps to position them over a certain track. Some use a worm gear or screw type shaft that moves the heads in and out. Others use solenoids. Solenoids are coils of wire that may be moved back and forth over a magnet by applying the appropriate voltages. Solenoids seem to be one of the better ways to position the heads, and they give very fast access times.

FORMATTING A HARD DISK

If at all possible have your vendor format your hard disk for you. The controller cards are usually designed so that they will operate with several different types of hard disks. So most have DIP switches that must be set to configure your particular hard disk. There is usually some documentation that comes with the hard disk controller, but in most cases it is very difficult to understand, especially if you are a beginner. **You must do a low-level format before you can use the DOS command FORMAT on your hard disk. See your hard disk's manual.**

The AT has a controller that can control the 360 K, the 1.2 Mb, and one or two hard disks. There are several manufacturers, but the documentation that I have seen for setting up the disks with these controllers is very poor. So again, if at all possible, have your vendor format the disk for you.

When you buy an AT, you should get a diagnostic diskette with it. This diskette will have the routines for checking out your machine and setting it up. It is also needed to set or reset the clock on the mother board.

The diagnostic routine asks several questions, then configures the BIOS for that configuration. This part of the BIOS is in low power CMOS semiconductors and they are powered by a battery pack on the back panel of the computer, so this BIOS configuration is on all the time, even when the computer is turned off. If the batteries go too low to power the BIOS, there is a large capacitor that can power it for about 15 minutes, or the time it would take to replace the batteries.

The routine asks what type of hard disk you have. There are 15 different types that the AT supports, but you must tell it what type you have installed. I gave it the wrong type and it cost me a couple of hours and a trip to the dealer. The battery had to be disconnected, and then the capacitor needed about 20 minutes to drain off. Only then were we able to re-configure the system so that the hard disk could be accessed.

HARD CARDS

About two years ago, Quadram Corporation developed a 10 Mb hard disk drive on a card that could be plugged into any slot in a PC or XT. The disk itself was located on one half of the board and the controller and associated electronics was on the other half. It was priced at $1000.00. It was a fantastic idea. Anyone could add a 10 Mb hard disk to their system by simply removing the cover to their computer and plugging in a card in an empty slot. There were no cables to hook up, no controller to worry about and anyone could install it.

Almost overnight, Mountain Computer Company and several other companies came out with similar hard disks on a card, except that many of the other companies put a 20 Mb disk on the card and charged only a hundred dollars or so more than Quadram did for their 10 Mb system. The heavy competition has constantly driven the price down to where you can now buy a 20 Mb hard disk system on a plug-in card for less than $400.00.

Quadram has recently announced that they will be offering a 20 Mb card. Almost immediately afterward, Mountain Computer announced that they would be offering a 30 Mb hard disk on a plug-in card. Paramount, Upic and other companies now have 80 Mb plug-in cards.

These plug-in hard disks on a card offer some great advantages over a standard hard disk. For instance, each person who has access to a computer in a large office could have their own hard disk. They could be plugged in and removed as often as you wanted to. This would provide confidentiality and security of data.

The cards are also portable so that data could be generated on one computer, then the card could be un-plugged, taken home or across country, and plugged into another one.

HARD DISK BACKUP

As we said earlier, having several hundred programs at your fingertips can give you a great feeling of power. But if the disk should crash it could wipe out hundreds of hours of hard work and lose invaluable data. This is why it is important to back up your disks every so often.

There are several methods for backing up a disk. DOS has a BACKUP command that will let you use ordinary floppy diskettes to back up a system. But it can take quite a lot of time and about 30 diskettes to back up a 10 Mb system.

Several companies offer a tape system that is fairly fast, and a small cartridge can hold up to 60 megabytes. See Fig. 9-5.

With a special plug-in card, it is now possible to use a video tape recorder as a backup system. See Fig. 9-6.

I prefer to use a software package called FASTBACK for my backups. It uses floppy diskettes, but it has its own format and records at a fairly high density and can record about 450 K bytes on a 360 K diskette. It still takes about 20 diskettes and about ten minutes to back up 10 Mb, but once a backup has been made, the next time a backup is made this software will allow you to selectively backup only those files that have changed.

Fig. 9-5. A tape backup system from Western Digital. (Photo courtesy Western Digital.)

CD ROM Backups

The next generation of mass storage will no doubt be on Compact Disk Read Only Memory. These are small 5 1/4 inch disks that are read by laser technology. The Grolier Publishing Company has put a copy of the entire Encyclopedia Brittanica on a disk. It takes up about one fourth of the area on one side of the small disk. The whole encyclopedia can be searched in just a few seconds for any subject, sentence or word. See Fig. 9-7.

Worm Backups

Another laser system that is similar to the CD ROM is the Write Once Read Many times. This system allows you to write enormous amounts, up to gigabytes, of data on a small 5 1/4 inch plastic disk. At the present time, most large companies are storing their permanent records on magnetic tape, but the tape can deteriorate over the years and is vulnerable to magnetic fields. The records on a tape are recorded serially. If you were looking for a specific record, you might have to wind off several hundred feet of tape in order to access it. The data on a Worm disk can be searched and accessed in just seconds, and the plastic disks are much more durable than floppy diskettes or magnetic tape and they are immune to be being erased by magnetic fields.

There is a definite need for this type of permanent storage, but it

Fig. 9-6. A videotape backup system from Alpha Micro Corporation. You may buy their VCR or use your own with their plug-in board.

would also be nice if we could erase and change portions of the records like we can on a hard disk. Several companies are working on such systems and we will probably have them in a short time.

THE INEVITABLE FAILURES

We said earlier that a properly designed semiconductor would last almost forever because it has no moving parts to wear out. But disk drives, printers, keyboards and other mechanical devices all have a limited life. Most mechanical devices have a spec sheet that lists the Mean Time Before Failure (MTBF). Often the MTBF is a projected figure that some statistical type pulled out of the air. In any case, it is just an average, and while the average life span of a man is 72 years, some live to be 95, others die soon after birth. Similarly with computer equipment. Like a human being, with a little tender loving care, the life of your hard disk or printer can be prolonged to some extent.

Because of the limited life of mechanical devices you should be careful in buying used equipment.

Fig. 9-7. A CD ROM system that can be interfaced to a computer. The laser disc in the front can store the entire Cyclopedia Britannica on less than one fourth of its recording area. (Photo courtesy of Knowledgeset Corporation.)

Chapter 10

Memory and Multifunction Boards

The computer uses two types of memory, Random Access Memory (RAM) and Read Only Memory (ROM). ROM is unlike RAM in several respects. ROM is fixed, permanent memory. It is like a book that can only be read. RAM is like a notepad that can be written on, erased, and then written on again.

Programs and files are loaded into RAM while they are being edited or changed, or while the program is performing its function. RAM can be used for a print spooler or buffer, used as a RAM disk, or to hold memory resident programs.

When used as a RAM disk, it appears to the computer as just another floppy disk drive, but it is a much faster drive than even the fastest hard disk. There might be a slight problem if you have a hard disk and you add a RAM disk. Your computer assigns letters to the floppy disk drives first, then the hard disk drives. If you have a single drive, it will be called both A: and B: (B: is the virtual drive). If you have two floppies, they will still be called A: and B:, but B: will be an actual drive. If you have a hard disk drive, it will be called C:. If you add another floppy, the new floppy will be called C: and the hard disk will be renamed D:. The problem arises if you have several programs and files on your C: hard disk that refer to C:, and the C: suddenly becomes D:, then every time you try to run that program the computer will look for information on the C: floppy that probably will not be there. If you add a RAM disk or an extra floppy drive, you will have to revise those programs that call for C:.

Another important difference between ROM and RAM is that RAM is volatile. That is, it disappears when the power is turned off, the machine is rebooted, or you exit a program and another one is loaded into memory. Suppose you had a class of students and there were some very important instructions written on a blackboard. These instructions didn't change very often and applied to all the classes held in that room. To keep them from being erased, they were painted onto the blackboard. This is similar to ROM. The rest of the blackboard is used for instructions and regular operations during class. At the end of the period, these instructions are erased, leaving a clean board for the next class. This is similar to RAM.

MOTHER BOARD MEMORY

You could only install up to 256 K on the mother board of the original IBM and early clones. But as soon as 256 K chips were available, the clones quickly modified their mother boards to accept up to 640 K. The clone companies are small and can make a design change almost overnight. IBM is big and ponderous and takes some time to change. Almost two years later, IBM has finally modified the PC-XT mother board to accept the 256 K chips so that 640 K can be installed. Putting 640 K on the mother board frees up one of the slots that would have otherwise been needed for a memory board.

A short time ago, the largest selling boards were multifunction boards that made it possible to add up to 384 K of additional memory. The AST SIX-PAK multifunction board became the de facto standard. Hundreds of thousands were sold at about $600.00 each. Of course the clones are quick to recognize a good product so they began turning out copies at half the cost, then half that. Figure 10-1 shows a Paradise multifunction board with 384 K.

As we mentioned earlier almost all mother boards now sold have the limit of 640 K on board, and it appears that most people who have the

Fig. 10-1. This is a Paradise multifunction board with clock/calendar, 384 K of memory, serial port, a print spooler and RAM disk.

older PCs and XTs have already bought multifunction boards. So there isn't too much need for the extra memory cards any more. I saw clone multifunction boards for as little as $79.00 at a recent computer swap.

This $79.00 board had no memory installed, or 0 K, but it had a clock/calendar, a parallel port, a serial port and software for creating a RAM disk and print spooling. So for these features alone, the card was well worth the money.

WHY THE 640 K LIMIT?

Incidentally, 640 K is the magic number for the maximum amount of memory that the PC or PC-XT can address without special hardware or software. Also, because IBM wanted to retain the PC-AT compatibility with the PC and PC-XT, the PC-AT is also limited to 640 K of Real Address Mode memory, but in the Protected Mode it can address up to 16 Mb on expansion boards. The boards come with special software that allows the memory to be used as print buffers, very fast RAM disks or for almost any other need that you might have.

Memory is structured in a precise architectural system. The various sections have definite addresses that are similar to your city, street and house address. The IBM system reserves a section of addresses just above 640 K for some of its internal operations. At the time this design was decided on, 64 K seemed like a lot of memory, so reserving ten times as much seemed to be enough. How times have changed.

THE COST OF RAM

In 1982 64 K of memory cost over $100.00. A few months ago I got a real bargain when I paid $21.00 for nine chips to make 64 K of memory. I have recently seen the same 64 K advertised for 49 cents per chip, or $4.50 for 64 K. A few months ago a set of 256 K chips would have cost well over $100.00. Several companies are now selling them for as little as $2.50 each or $22.50 for the nine chips needed to make 256 K. Of course, these less expensive chips are the slower ones, at about 200 nanoseconds (ns). But this is fast enough for most PCs and XTs, especially those that run at 4.77 MHz. The faster turbo computers may require 150 ns or better.

HOW MUCH MEMORY DO YOU NEED?

This will depend primarily on what you intend to use your computer for. When you run a program, data is read from the disk into RAM and operated on there. You will definitely need at least 256 K for a program like dBASE III. Some spreadsheet programs like Lotus 1-2-3 use a tremendous amount of memory. dBASE and Lotus will each run more quickly with more than their minimum required memory, so 512 K or 640 K are advisable for them.

If you have one of the older PCs that is limited to 64 K, then you definitely need to buy a memory expansion card with room for 384 K on it. There are many programs that have become very user friendly, but the more friendly the software, the more memory it takes to run it.

Memory Residents

There is a need for memory for memory resident programs like Sidekick, Superkey, Prokey, WordFinder and others. They can be loaded into memory and will lurk in the background. They will then pop up with a window whenever needed.

EXPANDED MEMORY SPECIFICATIONS (EMS)

In a joint venture, the Intel Corporation and Lotus Corporation designed a plug-in board that can be populated with up to 2 Mb of RAM. A piggyback card can be added to this one for another 2 Mb. They called it the *Above Board* and set up some specifications which they called the Expanded Memory Specifications (EMS). See Fig. 10-2.

Depending on the configuration and the amount of installed memory, the Above Board can cost from $295.00 up to $1495.00. This board can be used on the PC, XT or AT. Several other American companies are now building similar cards for similar prices. You can be sure that the clones will be offering one that is similar to these, or better, in a very short time for about half the price.

The high capacity memory boards work best on the PC-AT, but many of them can be used on the PC-XT with special software.

There seems to be a corollary concerning computer memory that was stated rather well by Mr. Bob Howe, an analyst. He was quoted in Com-

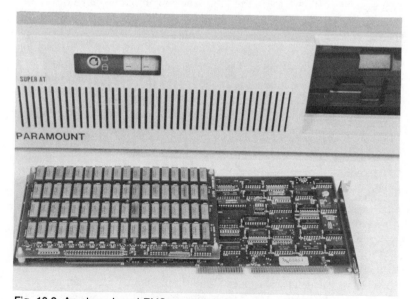

Fig. 10-2. An above-board EMS expansion card.

puter System News as saying, "Memory is like Heroin—users will always use more." Someone else stated another fact, "The need for memory will expand to whatever amount is available." Having lots of memory is like having a car with a large engine. You may not need that extra power very often, but it sure feels great being able to call on it when you do need it.

SPEED

All that power won't do much good if you have to chug along like a big semi that can't get out of first gear. A speed of 4.77 MHz (4.77 million cycles per second) may seem pretty fast. But there are some Computer Aided Design (CAD) programs, number crunching programs, and others that can be almost as slow as the traffic in Silicon Valley during commuting hours. If you have an XT with the turbo option, it can help to some extent. But the 8088 CPU is not a true 16 bit device so the speed is limited.

You can increase the speed some by removing the 8088 and installing a NEC V20. This newer CPU is internally structured somewhat differently from the 8088 and depending on the application you are running, it can increase the speed from 10 to as much as 30 percent. It costs between $10.00 and $20.00.

If you really want speed you need to replace the 8088 with an 8086 or 80186, or better yet, an 80286. These are all true 16 bit CPUs and handle data in 16 bit wide chunks. The 8088 processes data as two 8 bit chunks at a time. Unfortunately, you can't just pull out your 8088 and plug in a 16 bit CPU. It takes quite a lot of hardware, and in some cases, some software to do the job. Several companies have developed boards and software that can make an XT run even faster than an AT. These boards are known as *Turbo cards*.

Some of these boards run in tandem with your 8088. In others you have to remove the 8088 and plug in a connector from a cable.

If you are doing a lot of number crunching, you need to install an 8087, or 80287. These are *math coprocessor* chips, which take the load off of your 8088 or 80286 CPU by taking over mathematical operations.

MULTIFUNCTION BOARDS

In addition to the memory, some boards have other functions such as RAM disks, spoolers, ports and clocks. The prices vary from $250.00 with no added memory, up to $4000.00 with 8 Mb.

If you don't need the speed, or can't afford it, then buy one of the less expensive boards so that you can have a clock. You probably bought a system that has 640 K on board, in which case you don't need a multifunction board with extra memory, unless you plan to install one with special software and a very large amount of above board memory. You can buy a multifunction board with no memory, or 0 K, for about $75.00.

There are also clocks on a chip that can be plugged into an empty ROM socket. By doing it this way you don't use up one of your slots. These clocks cost about $60.00.

While your computer is running, everything it does is done by very precise timing that is crystal controlled. But when you turn off the power, this clock is idle. If you have a clock calendar, it usually has a small lithium or rechargeable battery on board that supplies power to the clock circuit when your computer is shut off. So when you turn it on the time and date is usually correct. So you can save a lot of keystrokes and time by not having to input the correct time and date each time you turn on your computer.

It is important that the correct time is input to the computer, because each time you create a file, the time and date is recorded with it. If you have to make a backup of your files, you can tell most backup systems to backup only those files that have changed since your last backup, so that it will compare the dates and time, then backup only the last files created or changed.

It is also necessary to determine just when a file was created for other reasons. If you have a hundred files on separate disks, knowing when they were created might give you a hint as to what is on them, or tell you whether they are the latest version. For businesses, the date of a transaction or account creation is very important.

Having a real time clock in your computer is also very handy. You can ask for the time or the date any time at the > by simply typing in the command TIME or DATE. It will pop up on your screen immediately. It is even possible to have the time and date displayed on the screen. There are several software programs that can do this. You can do it yourself by using the PROMPT command. For instance:

C > PROMPT $p td$g

This command will tell you what directory you are in, the time that you entered it and the date. The time will not change, in this case, until the next time the prompt is displayed. With the little program above you might see this:

C \ WS 7:40:02.80 Fri 7-18-86 >

If you wait a short time and press the return key again, you will get an updated time similar to this:

C \ WS 7:43:50.32 Fri 7-18-86 >

The time will change to the hundredths of a second each time you press the return.

The example prompt above tells you what directory you are in and what time and the date that you entered it. You could do a PrtSc (Print Screen) of this and then go to another directory, and then come back and be able to know exactly how much time was spent on a project.

SOURCES

Here is a list of a few companies that make multifunction and accelerator boards for the PC, the XT and the AT. This is not a complete list:

AST Research,
2121 Alton Av.,
Irvine, CA 92714

Basic Time,
3350 Scott, Bldg. 52,
Santa Clara, CA 95054

Boca Research,
6401 Congress Av.
Boca Raton, FL 33431

Emulex/Persyst,
3545 Harbor Blvd.,
Costa Mesa, CA 92626

Everex Systems,
47777 Warm Springs Blvd.,
Fremont, CA 94539

IDEAssociates,
35 Dunham Rd.,
Billerica, MA 01821

MA Systems,
2015 O'Toole Av.,
San Jose, CA 95131

Maynard,
460 E. Semoran Blvd.,
Casselberry, FL 32707

Orchid Tech.,
44790 Westinghouse Dr.,
Fremont, CA 94539

Paradise,
217 E. Grand Av.
So. San Francisco, CA 94080

Quadram,
One Quad Way,
Norcross, GA 30093

Sigma Designs,
2023 O'Toole Av.,
San Jose, CA 95131

STB,
601 N. Glenville,
Richardson, TX 75080

Tall Tree,
1120 San Antonio Rd., #124
Palo Alto, CA 94303

Tecmar,
6225 Cochran Rd.,
Solon, OH 44139

Univation,
1231 California Circle,
Milpitas, CA 95035

Vutek,
10855 Sorrento Valley Rd.,
San Diego, CA 92121

Chapter 11

Monitors

Many of the ads that you see for computers are quite misleading. Often they will show a complete system, but they may not tell you that the monitor is extra until you get down to the store. Actually the computer can be operated without a monitor. The monitor only reflects, or echoes, the data that is being sent to the computer innards, but if you don't have a monitor, it is somewhat like trying to find your way around in a totally dark room, except that you don't even know when you've bumped into a wall. Figure 11-1 shows a couple of monitors.

Basically, a monitor is similar to a television set. The face of a tv set or a monitor is the end of a Cathode Ray Tube (CRT). They are vacuum tubes and have many of the same elements that made up the old radio and electronic vacuum tubes that were used before the advent of the semiconductor age. The CRT's have a filament that lets off a stream of electrons. The back of the CRT face has a voltage of about 25,000 volts. This pulls the stream of electrons to the face where they slam into the phosphor on the back side and cause it to light up.

To get to the front of the tube, this stream of electrons must pass between a system of electrically charged plates. In a basic system there would be a plate on the left, one on the right, one at the top and one at the bottom. The plates can be activated so that the beam of electrons are repulsed by one side and attracted by the other, or pulled to the top or forced to the bottom.

Fig. 11-1. A NEC high resolution monitor on the left and my original Taxan standard resolution monitor. You can't tell just by looking what a world of difference there is between the images on these two screens.

These plates can manipulate the beam of electrons to start writing at the top left corner of the CRT, move all the way across to the top right corner, then move back to the left side and drop down one line and write another line across the screen. It does this very fast and soon fills the entire screen.

The CRT also has control grids, as did the old vacuum tubes, for signal input. The signal can modify the beam of electrons so that none or only a few are allowed to get through. The control grid, along with the electromagnetic system, causes the electron stream to emulate the input signal and write it on the screen.

If you look at a photo from a newspaper with a magnifying glass, you can see that the picture is made up of dots. Some of the dots are not quite as dark as the others which gives the picture shading and definition. The electron beam creates images in much the same way. As a beam moves across the screen it is turned on and off so that only certain pixels are caused to light up.

A color system has three electron beams, one each for the Red, Green and Blue (RGB). The monochrome CRT has a single color phosphor, usually green or amber. The color CRT has many small dots of red, green and blue placed close to each other. These three primary colors can be blended to create any shade or color. The electron beams are directed to the three different colored dots and cause them to light up with varying intensity to create colors and images.

If you would like to see what the dots look like, take a fairly strong magnifying glass and look at some text or graphics on a color screen.

The white letters will have all of the colors lit up. If there is a blue or red or green color on the screen, only those dots for that color will be lit. Of course if it is black, none of them will be lit.

It is possible to use a tv set as a monitor. You would need a modula-'tor that attaches to the tv antenna. Usually, they are tuned to channel 3 of the tv. There are several disadvantages to using a tv as a monitor. A computer monitor will display 80 characters or columns across it. A tv set will only display 40 characters. The characters will be spread out and be rather difficult to read. Using a tv as a monitor might be all right for games and simple graphics, but it would not be suitable for any kind of serious computing.

Some of the less expensive monitors have a composite input. They don't have the RGB inputs. The input is through a single RCA type input jack.

RESOLUTION

Since the monochrome CRT's have only one color phosphor, the pixels are usually very close together. The color monitors have three different dots that must be lit up by beams from three different guns. For instance, the red dots are separated by the green and blue dots, so the resolution is not as good in the standard color monitors as in the monochrome.

There are some high resolution color monitors. Naturally, the higher the resolution, the higher the cost. To manufacture a higher resolution color monitor, smaller dots of red, green and blue phosphors are deposited on the screen, but the smaller dots mean that the beams must be more accurately aimed so that they will impinge correctly on their own particular color. The manufacture of the high resolution monitors demands much closer tolerances. This makes them more costly to build than monochrome monitors.

DOT PITCH

The color monitor has a perforated mask called a shadow mask. This mask filters the three different electron beams so that they strike only their color. The space between the perforations is called the dot pitch. The smaller the spacing, the higher the resolution. A typical medium resolution would be .38. A high resolution would be .31 or less.

If you look at the characters or images on a low resolution monitor you can see open spaces. A high resolution monitor will have good, solid, sharply defined letters and images. Difference is somewhat like the print of a low cost dot matrix printer as compared to a good letter quality one.

SCANNING FREQUENCY

The horizontal scanning frequency of a standard tv set is 15.75 kHz. Many monitors use the same frequency, but the better ones may have a frequency up to 35 kHz or more.

ADAPTORS

You cannot simply plug a computer into a monitor and have it work. It must have an interface. These interfaces are called display adaptors. Figure 11-2 shows an adaptor card.

A whole book could be written about adaptors. There are three basic types, the Monochrome Display Adaptor (MDA), the Color/Graphics Adaptor (CGA), and the Enhanced Graphics Adaptor (EGA). Some of the adaptors may have other built-in functions such as a parallel or a serial port for printers and modems.

The adaptors set the monitors up so that they will display 80 characters across the screen on a single line and they will display 25 lines from top to bottom. So that means that the maximum number of characters or spaces that can be typed and displayed on a screen is $80 \times 25 = 2000$. The computer considers each one of those 2000 spaces to be a block and the screen is laid out in grid arrangement much like a sheet of graph paper. Each one of those blocks has an address starting at 0 to 79 for the first line across the top and 0 to 24 for each line down. The address of the block in the upper left corner is row 0, column 0; the block in the lower right corner is row 24, column 79. Software programs can send the cursor to any block on the screen.

Characters are formed within the area of each of those 2000 blocks by causing the electron beam to strike the phosphor or picture elements (pixels) within that block. The medium resolution monitors have 320 pixels or dots across the face of the screen and 200 pixels from the top to the bottom. This gives a total of 64,000 pixels for the entire screen. The high resolution monitor has 640 pixels across and 200 from top to bottom for a total of 128,000. Enhanced Graphics Adaptors (EGA) may allow 640×350 for a total of 224,000 pixels. The monochrome adapters can have a resolution of 720×350 for a total of 252,000.

Fig. 11-2. A CGA monitor card. Note the "skirt" on the card. Except for the small notch the board extends to the same level as the bottom of the connectors. This board could only be used in slot 2 or 6 of an AT because of the 16 bit connectors in front of the other slots.

A dot matrix type system is used to form the characters or images. To find the number of pixels in an individual block on a monitor with 640 × 200, we would divide the 640 by the 80 columns to get 8; we would then divide the 200 vertical pixels by the 25 lines to get 8. So each block would have 8 × 8 for a total of 64 pixels. There is a certain amount of space that must be left around each character, so the character created within an 8 × 8 block is formed from a 5 × 7 matrix. A high resolution monochrome monitor with 720 × 350 pixels would have a block made up of 9 × 14. The dot-matrix character created within one of these blocks would be 7 pixels high by 9 wide.

SUPER HIGH RESOLUTION AND EGA

It won't do you any good to buy a high resolution color monitor unless you have a high resolution adaptor. IBM was one of the first to offer an Enhanced Graphic Adaptor (EGA). Its price is $995.00. A high resolution monitor was offered to go with the EGA for $895.00.

Several American vendors are now offering an EGA for about half of the cost of the IBM EGA. The Far East clone makers are offering them for about $250.00, or about half of what the American suppliers are asking. An EGA card is shown in Fig. 11-3.

A good high resolution color monitor may cost from $500.00 on up to several thousand. It is possible to get a standard resolution monitor for about $300 and up. Some monochromes are selling for as little as $100.00.

There are several monitors that are in the super high resolution range. This range would be about 700 × 400 or more. They require an EGA

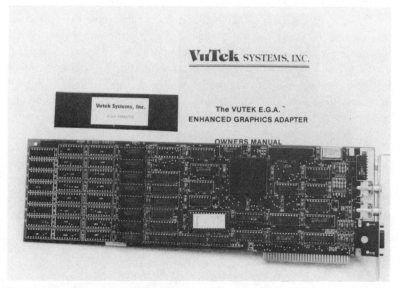

Fig. 11-3. An EGA card from VuTek.

103

in order to display this resolution. They are fairly reasonable in cost, from $500.00 up to $800.00.

There are professional models of monitors that can generate over 1024 × 1024 resolution. The screens may be as large as 19 inches. The cost may be $10,000.00 or more. These monitors require a Professional Enhanced Graphics Adaptor (PEGA) to drive them. The cost of the PEGA may be $3000.00 or more. These units are usually bought for Computer Aided Design/Computer Aided Manufacturing (CAD/CAM) programs.

WHAT SHOULD YOU BUY

If you can afford it, buy a good super high resolution color monitor and an EGA. If you expect to do any kind of graphics, it will be a great improvement. But if you are only going to use it for word processing and maybe a few database and BASIC programs, then the high resolution monochrome will do fine.

If you can, go to a computer show and look at the various types available. Or go to several stores and compare them. Turn the brightness up and check the center of the screen and the outer edges. Is the intensity the same in the center and the outer edges? There can be differences, no matter whose name is on the unit. There are two IBM color display monitors at the office where I work. The focus is off on one of them. It has been sent back twice, but it is still not right.

Ask the vendor for a copy of the specs. Check the dot pitch. If it is a high resolution, it should be .38 or less. A super high resolution should have .31 or less. Check the pixel resolution. A high resolution should be about 640 × 200. A super high resolution should be about 700 or more × 400 or more. Check for available buttons or knobs to control and adjust the brightness, contrast and vertical/horizontal lines.

Of course you should buy an adaptor to fit your monitor. A monochrome adaptor (MDA) will drive only monochrome monitors. They will cost about $100.00. If you want monochrome graphics capability, it will cost about $200.00. A Color Graphics Adaptor (CGA) will drive anything, from a monochrome up to a high resolution monitor, but not necessarily at its highest resolution. It will cost about $100.00. An Enhanced Graphics Adapter will drive almost any kind of monitor and will cost $250.00 and up.

RESOLUTION STANDARDS

There are no standards as to what comprises high, medium, low or super high resolution. Charles Petzold, writing in the PC Magazine, suggested that the following be adopted as standard:

RESOLUTION	OLD TERM	NEW TERM
650 × 350	Enhanced	Medium Res.
640 × 200	High Res.	Low Res.
320 × 200	Medium Res.	Very Low Res.
160 × 200	Low Res.	No Res.

Prices continue to come down. There is little doubt that soon you will be able to buy a 19 inch monitor with 1024 × 1024 resolution for about what a 13 inch 650 × 350 costs today.

Personally, I enjoy working with color. I am willing to do without a whole lot of other things in order to have it.

Here are a few of the EGA board vendors. This list is by no means complete:

AST Research
2121 Alton Av.
Irvine, CA 92714

ATronics
491 Valley Way, Bldg. 1
Milpitas, CA 95035

Emulex/Persyst
3545 Harbor Blvd.
Costa Mesa, CA 92626

Everex
48431 Milmont Dr.,
Fremont, CA 94538

Genoa Systems
73 E. Trimble Rd.
San Jose, CA 95131

IDEAssociates
35 Dunham Rd.
Billerica, MA 01821

NSI Logic
257-B Cedar Hill Rd.
Marlboro, MA 01752

Paradise
217 E. Grand Av.
So. San Francisco, CA 94080

PC Designs
11105-B E. 56th St.
Tulsa, OK 74146

Quadram Co.
One Quad Way
Norcross, GA 30093

Sigma
110 N. Miller Av.
Anaheim, CA 92806

STB Systems
601 N. Glenville
Richardson, TX 75080

Tecmar
6225 Cochran Rd.
Solon, OH 44139

Tseng Labs
205 Pheasant Run
Newtown, PA 18940

Video-7
550 Sycamore Dr.
Milpitas, CA 95035

Vutek
10855 Sorrento Valley Rd.
San Diego, CA 92121

Chapter 12

Printers

Choosing a printer can be quite a problem. There are so many factors to consider. The first thing to consider, of course, is what do you want to do with it. Do you need speed, letter-quality, graphics, tractor feed, wide carriage, or all of the above? Do you want IBM graphics compatibility? Do you have a lot of money to spend?

TYPES OF PRINTERS

There are two main types of printers, dot-matrix and letter-quality. Dot-matrix is usually faster than letter-quality.

Dot-Matrix

The print head of a dot-matrix printer has a vertical row of pins. Some of the less expensive printers have only 7 pins, the more expensive ones may have as many as 24. As the head moves in finite increments across the paper, solenoids push individual pins forward to form characters. (Note: The solenoids in a print head generate a powerful magnetic field. Do not place your floppy disks near them while they are printing.)

Here is a representation of the pins in a 7 pin print head and how it would form the letter A:

```
1 •              •
2 •           •  •
3 •          •     •
4 •        •         •
5 •      • •••••••• •
6 •         •      •
7 •           •      •
```

The print head moves from left to right.

The numbered dots on the left represent the individual pins in the head before it starts moving across the paper.

The 7-dot matrix may be rather difficult to read. Some of the characters such as the y, p, q and g may not descend below the line. The more expensive dot-matrix printers may have as many as 24 pins. The pins will be smaller and the printed dots will be closer together. The characters may even be Near Letter Quality (NLQ). Some achieve NLQ by printing the character once, then slightly off-setting the print head and printing over it a second time. This cuts the speed of the printer down by about half, of course.

In draft mode (with NLQ turned off), most dot-matrix printers can print at about 150 to 200 characters per second (cps). Draft quality is often sufficient for such things as informal notes, memos and preliminary reports.

A quick draft copy makes proof reading and editing much easier than trying to do it on the computer. Most monitors have twenty five lines only. And many word processors use 10 to 15 of those lines for menus and help, which means you can only see a small portion of the page at any one time. You might make a correction or amendment on the portion of the page that is showing on the screen, then completely forget about it when the other half of the page comes up. So it's best to print out a quick rough draft and do your proofing on a hard copy. When you have made all the necessary changes and polished it into a real gem, then use the slower NLQ mode.

Many of the better dot-matrix printers can print several different font styles and sizes. There are several software programs that can be used to print out signs, banners and all sorts of graphics.

Most of the better dot-matrix printers today use a 24 pin head that can give near letter quality printing at about 100 cps. They print draft quality at up to 300 cps. Most of them emulate the Epson or IBM character set, and many will accept character sets and fonts that can be downloaded from supplied software. A few of them use multi-color ribbons that can print out up to seven colors.

The price of a dot-matrix printer will depend on the speed, functions and other goodies that you want on it. You can buy an acceptable one for about $175.00. Better ones may cost from $300.00 up to $3000.00.

Letter-Quality

Most of the letter-quality printers use a daisy wheel, a thimble, or

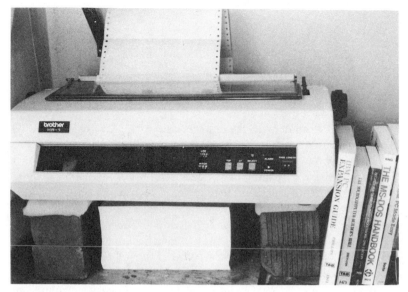

Fig. 12-1. My Brother HR-1 daisy-wheel printer.

some other device that has formed characters on it. Compared to dot-matrix printers, they are very slow. They usually print from 10 to 45 cps. As a daisy wheel spins a solenoid pushes a pin or hammer forward to strike the individual characters and push them against the ribbon and paper, typing just as a typewriter does. The daisy wheel continues to spin as the characters are being hit. It takes precise timing for the hammer to hit a character and release it while the wheel is spinning. So you can see why most letter-quality printers are rather slow. Figure 12-1 shows my old Brother HR-1 which types at about 15 characters per second.

The wheels, thimbles or other devices are usually limited to about 100 characters. There is usually only one font style and type of print on each device. However, it is usually possible to have several different wheels with different fonts and sizes. To change to a different font style or print size, you must stop the printer and change the wheel or other device. Figure 12-2 shows a couple of drop-in daisy wheels.

The price of these printers depends on the speed, functions and the bells and whistles that you may want to add. A fairly good one may cost as little as $300.00. The better ones may cost up to $2000.00.

Which Is Better

The better dot-matrix printers offer near letter quality, high speed, the ability to download various fonts from the computer and the ability to do graphics. Because of these advantages over the daisy-wheel printers, many prefer the dot-matrix printers for a general purpose printer, but not all dot-matrix printers can do all of the functions mentioned above.

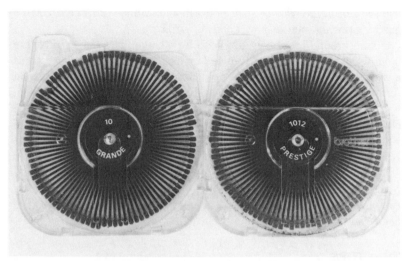

Fig. 12-2. A couple of the drop in daisy wheels with different type fonts.

By all means get a sample printout. If you expect to do any graphics, or use any software that might use the expanded character set, find out if the printer has a character set that is compatible with the Epson and IBM printers.

There are many more dot-matrix printers sold than letter-quality printers, but the daisy wheel is not quite dead yet. Near letter quality is not good enough for most formal business letters, which must look like they were typed on a very expensive typewriter. It will probably be some time before the daisy wheel disappears completely.

RIBBONS

Most dot-matrix printers use a nylon cloth ribbon. They are relatively inexpensive and can last for quite a long time. Most ribbons cost between four and ten dollars each. But there are kits available that can be used to re-ink the ribbons. After the kit is paid for, it costs only pennies to re-ink a ribbon, and they can be used over and over until the fabric wears out.

You can also prolong the life of a ribbon for a short time by spraying it with the lubricant WD-40 and let it sit for a while. There is a narrow margin along the edges of the cloth ribbon that is never struck. The WD-40 dissolves this ink and lets it blend across the ribbon. It is sometimes difficult to get the spray inside a cartridge to reach all of the ribbon. You can sometimes take the cover off of the cartridge, but if you are not careful, you will have ribbon all over the room. A ribbon treated with WD-40 will not last as long or have the print quality of a new ribbon, but in an emergency, it is better than nothing.

Many of the letter-quality printers use a carbon film type of ribbon. This gives good crisp letters that are very high quality. It is possible to use the cloth type ribbons, but cloth ribbons cannot produce the same quality print, no matter how good the printer is.

The carbon film ribbons are good for a single pass only. And there is no way that they can be re-inked or used again. Some printers use a wide ribbon in a cartridge. My old Brother HR-1 uses a 5/8" carbon film ribbon that is the same as the ones used by the IBM Selectric typewriters. The ribbon carriage moves the ribbon up and down so that three characters can be struck across the width of the ribbon. One of these ribbons will allow several thousand characters to be printed in a single pass.

Both cloth and carbon film ribbons are available in various colors. Most ribbons are on cartridges that are very easy to change, so it is fairly easy to stop the printer and change colors when you want to. A little color can be a great way to grab attention or to emphasize a point.

TRACTORS

Most of the printers offer a tractor feed, usually as an option. A tractor is a pair of spiked wheels that are used with the holes on each side of computer paper. The tractor insures that the paper is fed at a constant rate. If you are trying to print labels or any document where the printing must line up, a tractor is essential.

I bought a tax program last year called PC TaxCut. When all the calculations are completed, they give you an IRS approved form that can be inserted into a printer. But if you don't have a tractor, the friction feed platen will usually slip a little so that by the end of the report none of the figures will be in their proper boxes.

Up until just recently, computer paper with the tractor holes was not really suitable for business letters and formal reports. When the margins with the holes were torn off the perforations left a ragged edge. Several companies are now selling a computer paper that is heavy bond and the edges are laser cut. The margins tear off evenly and leave no indication of perforations.

LASER PRINTERS

Laser printers have been around for quite a while. Some of the early ones cost as much as $100,000.00. Then Cannon developed one that cost around $10,000.00, and a short time later Hewlett-Packard came out with their Laserjet that cost about $3600.00. The QMS Company of Mobile Alabama has recently offered one for $1995.00. The HP Laserjet is now being advertised for less than $2500.00. See Figs. 12-3 and 12-4.

Laser printers combine laser and reproduction machine technologies. A laser writes the characters on a large rotating drum that is similar to the ones used in photocopy machines. This drum can then print a whole sheet of paper in one rotation.

The laser printers can print several different font styles, type sizes

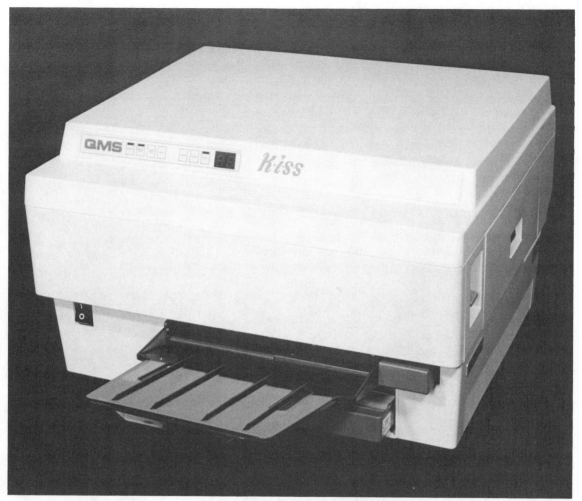

Fig. 12-3. A relatively inexpensive laser printer from QMS Corporation. (Photo courtesy QMS Corp.)

and graphics. They can print from six to over ten pages per minute.

As I am writing this, several companies are working to develop a color laser printer. QMS is expected to announce one soon. Laser color will be rather expensive at first, probably around $25,000. But like most of the other innovations in the computer world, the price will no doubt come down as soon as the clone makers can start producing them.

PRINTER NOISE

Laser printers are fairly quiet. Dot-matrix and letter-quality printers can be very loud. If you are working nearby and trying to concentrate they can be distracting and irritating. They can be enclosed in sound proofing boxes that are lined with foam rubber. This reduces the noise by a considerable amount.

PRINTER STANDS

Several companies have stands for printers. These stands let the printer sit up five or six inches above the table or desk. The folded continuous sheets of paper can then be placed underneath and fed to the printer. These stands may cost from $20.00 to $40.00.

I never seem to have enough money, so I am always looking for ways to save. I took my large letter-quality printer and made a stand out of four bricks so that I could put the paper under it. I put some foam rubber between the bricks and the printer and it reduced the noise by over fifty percent. If you look back at Fig. 12-1 you can see the bricks and foam rubber.

BUFFERS AND BAUD RATES

A computer can feed data to a printer thousands of times faster than the fastest printer can operate. Ordinarily, if your computer is sending a document to the printer, you can't use your computer for anything else

Fig. 12-4. The LaserJet printer from Hewlett-Packard. (Photo courtesy Hewlett-Packard.)

until the printing is finished.

Some of the older printers have built-in buffers of 1 K to 4 K or more of memory. As the printer moves the data out of the buffer and prints it, the computer sends in more until the document is completed. Since the cost of memory has come way down, many of the newer printers are adding much larger buffers from 8 K to 16 K or more. With a large buffer, the computer can send a whole file very quickly and then be available for other uses.

PRINT SPOOLERS

There are several multifunction boards such as the AST and Paradise boards that come with print spooler software programs. These programs allocate a portion of the computer's RAM memory as a printer buffer. A file can then be sent to this RAM memory and fed to the printer as needed. Your computer is then free to do other tasks.

EXTERNAL BUFFERS

There are some programs that cannot use a print spooler, so they must have an external buffer. These are small boxes that are plugged in between the computer and the printer. They may have from 16 K of memory up to 500 K or more.

NO STANDARDS

One of the programmers where I work spent months developing a database program that would print out some simple graph charts and forms. His computer had an Okidata printer attached to it so the program was written to run on that printer. It was run, re-run and polished until it ran perfectly.

But when the end user tried to print the charts out on a Toshiba printer it went crazy. The program had to be completely rewritten because the graphics print character sets of the two printers are completely different.

WordStar 2000 lists over 200 different printers that it supports. But that list is not nearly complete. Every one of those printers are different in some way. There is no standard among them whatsoever.

THE IBM AND EPSON STANDARD

For several years, IBM bought a small Japanese made Epson dot-matrix printer and put their name on it. It was a good little printer and was capable of printing out graphics. IBM adopted the Epson character set and it has become somewhat standard, although not nearly as widely accepted as it should be. Many of the commercial graphics software packages do use the Epson character set. So if you plan to print out any graphics, try to find a printer that has the Epson character set.

INTERFACES

Printers can be very difficult to interface. There are two types of printer interfaces, serial and parallel. In the serial system the bits are transmitted serially, one bit at a time. The parallel system uses an eight line bus and eight bits are transmitted at a time, one bit on each line at a time. It takes eight bits to make one character, so with the parallel system, a whole character can be transmitted on the eight lines at one time.

The parallel system was developed by the Centronics Company. IBM adopted the parallel system as the default mode for their PC and PC-XT. Of course the clones followed suit, and so parallel inputs are the standard on most printers sold today. Many printers will accept parallel or serial. You can buy printer boards with a parallel or serial output port. Some boards provide both. Be sure to determine what your printer requires before you buy a printer board.

The RS232C Standard

The RS232C standard was developed to connect Data Terminal Equipment (DTE), and Data Communication Equipment (DCE). Usually the computer is designated as the DTE and the printer or modem as the DCE. Table 12-1 is a brief description of the signals and their direction and function.

As you can see, this standard looks fairly simple. Most of the boards that are manufactured for the IBM PC and compatibles will have the RS232 ports wired as Data Terminal Equipment or DTE. But many of the printer and peripheral equipment manufacturers ignore this standard. Some may wire the printer as the DTE and others as a DCE. Still other manufacturers may use a combination of the two. Before you buy a cable for your printer or modem, try to determine what configuration you will need. Cables may cost from $25.00 to well over $55.00. A specially made cable may cost over $100.00. If you shop around you can buy the connectors and the wire for less than $10.00, and make a cable yourself.

Table 12-1. Standard Serial Port Connections.

Pin #	Direction	Function
1		Chassis ground
2	DTE − − > DCE	TX transmit data to DCE
3	DTE < − − DCE	RX receive data from DCE
4	DTE − − > DCE	RTS request to send data
5	DTE < − − DCE	CTS clear to send data
20	DTE − − > DCE	DTR data terminal ready
6	DTE < − − DCE	DSR data set ready
7		Signal ground
8	DTE < − − DCE	Data carrier detect

Table 12-2. Standard Wiring for a Parallel Printer Cable.

Printer			Printer
DB25 Pin #	Assignment		Centronics Pin #
1	Strobe	– – >	1
2	Data 0	– – >	2
3	Data 1	– – >	3
4	Data 2	– – >	4
5	Data 3	– – >	5
6	Data 4	– – >	6
7	Data 5	– – >	7
8	Data 6	– – >	8
9	Data 7	– – >	9
10	Acknow.	< – –	10
11	Busy	< – –	11
12	Paper end	< – –	12
13	Select	< – –	13
14	Auto feed	– – >	14
15	Error	< – –	15
16	Init.	– – >	16
17	Sel. Inp.	– – >	17
18-25	Ground		18-25

The Parallel System

The parallel port will usually have a DB25 type connector that is the same as the serial port. So it may be difficult to determine whether a connector is parallel or serial by just looking at it. Sometimes, but not always, the parallel and serial ports will be of opposite sex. That is to say, that one will have pins and the other will have sockets to accept a cable with pins. You would have to look at the board that the connector is mounted on. You might even have to have the board's original documentation to determine what kind of port it has. When you do determine what kind of port it is, mark it so that there can be no mistake.

The printer will almost always have a Centronics type connector. These connectors usually have spring clips that hold the mating connector in place. Table 12-2 is a listing of the usual pin assignments from the computer to a DB25 connector to a Centronics.

PRINTER PROBLEMS

My original computer, a little Morrow CP/M machine, had a single serial output port built onto the main board. I bought a Brother HR-1 serial printer for it. I had a bit of trouble modifying the cable for it because the Brother did not conform to the RS232 standards and neither did the Morrow output port, but once I found the right combination, it worked fine. A couple of years later I had problems again when I tried to interface my IBM compatible clone to my Brother printer. I had to take my printer cable apart and change some of the wires around again.

After I was satisfied that I had changed the wires in the cable to the proper pins, I tried to plug in my printer. It was then that I first noticed that the printer cable and the output connector on the computer both had male pins. Several companies make gender changer DB-25 connectors. This is simply two male or two female connectors wired back to back. They are advertised at discount houses for around $10.00 each. The only store near me that had one wanted $27.00 for it, so I bought a female connector, cut off one end of my cable and wired it on. There are 25 pins in these connectors, but, depending on the printer, as few as three may be used. My printer uses ten lines.

As we said earlier, the IBM and clones default to the parallel printer port. This means that when the computer is turned on it will use the parallel port for printing unless told otherwise. My printer is a serial unit. To use the serial output port, I had to use the MODE command as follows:

    MODE COM1:1200,N,8,P.

Then

    MODE LPT1:=COM1.

The 1200 sets the baud rate to 1200, the N means No parity, the 8 means 8 bits, the P means to send the output to the Printer. The baud rate for some printers may be from 300 to 9600 or more. The parity can be none, one or two, the bits are usually 8, but may be 7. The output could be directed to a modem or to some device other than the printer. The second MODE command means that LPT1 or LinePrinTer1 will be connected to the COM1 output port.

The computer will remain in this mode unless a subsequent MODE command is issued to change it, or the computer is turned off or re-booted. So that I wouldn't have to go through the trouble of typing in this command every time I turned on my computer, I put the MODE command in my AUTOEXEC.BAT file. This automatically loads the command each time the computer is turned on. Your own printer may require a different parity or bit path than mine, so be sure to check the manual.

Interfacing is only one of the possible problems that you can have with printers. Since they contain many moving mechanical parts that are subject to wear, you can be sure that sooner or later they will require some attention. As I am writing this, my Brother HR-1 is in the repair shop. After three years of hard use, the small motor that reels the printer ribbon onto the takeup spool has failed.

The local computer service shop owner said that most of his business is repairing printers. He charges $50.00 an hour plus parts. Most jobs require at least two hours labor. I had to wait three weeks before he got the parts. It cost me $237.00 for parts and labor. If my printer lasts another three years that won't be too bad, but if it goes down again soon I will probably scrap it and buy a new one.

OTHER TYPES OF PRINTERS

There are several other types of printers that are available. Thermal printers are relatively inexpensive. They use heat to darken a specially treated paper. They are quieter than the impact type dot-matrix printers but their quality is rather poor. Ink jet printers spray ink onto the paper to form characters. They are quiet, since there is no impact. They are also capable of printing in various colors.

PLOTTERS

Plotters are devices that can draw almost any shape or design under the control of a computer. A plotter may have from one to seven different colored pens. Though shorter, the pens are quite similar to ball point pens. Figures 12-5, 12-6 and 12-7 show some of the different types of plotters.

The plotter arm can be directed to choose any one of the various

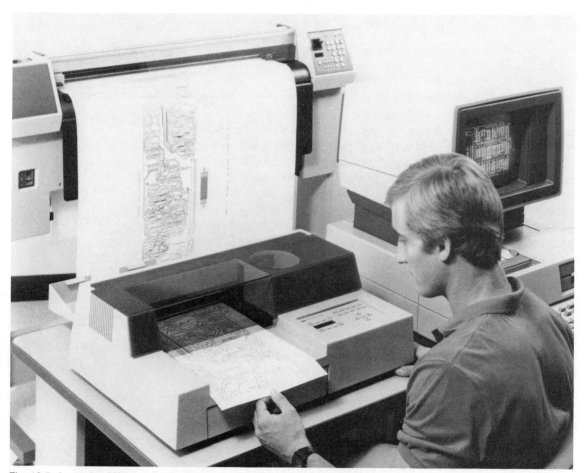

Fig. 12-5. A couple of Hewlett-Packard plotters. (Photo courtesy Hewlett- Packard.)

Fig. 12-6. A relatively inexpensive plotter from Houston Instruments. (Photo courtesy Houston Instruments.)

pens and to trace out any design. On most plotters, the arm is controlled by a motor that can move it in very small increments from side to side, while another motor moves the paper from top to bottom. On some plotters the paper remains still, and the pen can move both vertically and horizontally. In either case, this ability to move freely in both directions enables the pen to draw lines of any shape you can define.

The pen is moved to defined X-Y coordinates. Each position on the paper is defined by two numbers; one for its horizontal position (X), and one for its vertical position (Y). For example, if the lower left corner is position 0-0, and the upper right corner of the paper is position 100-100, then the center point of the paper would be position 50-50.

With a system like this, and a computer program that can control plotters, the plotter can draw graphs or images, do letter-quality lettering, make presentation transparencies, and draw almost any kind of design that you want. All of this can be done in as many as seven different colors.

There are many very good graphics programs available for plotters. If you are doing design work, need a sign made up, or need a set of transparencies for a presentation, then you need a plotter. One of the disadvantages of plotters is that they are rather slow.

Depending on the bells and whistles and goodies that you may want, a plotter may cost from $200 up to several thousand.

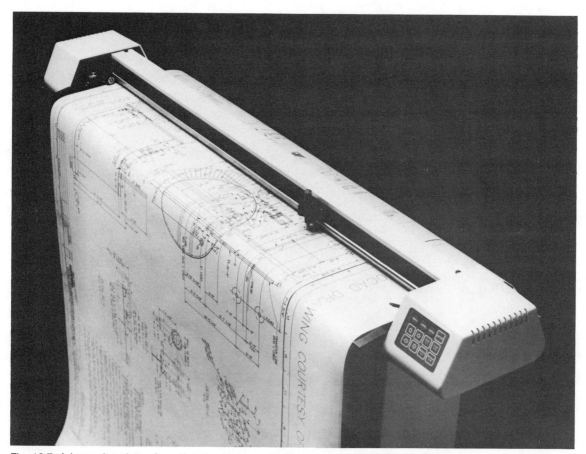

Fig. 12-7. A large size plotter from Houston Instruments (Photo courtesy Houston Instruments.)

Chapter 13

Modems

With a modem, your computer can talk to any number that can be called on your telephone, if there is a computer with a modem on the other end. Modem is an acronym of the words MOdulate-DEModulate. Computers send out digital signals of zeroes and ones. The telephone system is set up to carry sound or voice in an analog signal. Analog means that the signal is electrically analogous, or similar in form to the sound waves made when we talk. The electrical signals in a telephone vary continuously, following the volume and pitch of our voices, while the electrical signals in a computer are discrete signals that are either on (1) or off (0). The modem modulates the digital signals and converts them into a form that can be transmitted over the phone lines. At the other end, a modem demodulates this signal and converts it back to digital information.

If you don't believe that you need a modem, it is probably only because you have never used one, or don't realize the many benefits it can provide. We are going to list just a few.

PUBLIC DOMAIN SOFTWARE

The initial cost of a computer can be insignificant compared to the cost of software that you might need. But it doesn't have to be that way.

Most of the popular commercial software packages cost from $150.00 to $750.00. But for most of the commercial packages there is an equivalent *public domain* program that will do almost everything that the com-

120

mercial package does. There are programs for word processing, spreadsheets, databases, computer utilities, communications programs, games, and almost any other need that you could possibly have. Quite often they are even better and more sophisticated than the high priced commercial packages, and one of the best things about the public domain software packages is that they are free. All you need to get these thousands of free programs is a telephone and a modem.

If you don't have a modem or don't have the time to download the programs you want, or can't find what you want, there are public domain publishers who will send you a diskette full of programs for a very nominal fee. Here are the addresses of a couple that are in my area:

MicroCom Systems
P.O. Box 51657
Palo Alto, CA 94303

PC SIG Library
1030D East Duane Ave.
Sunnyvale, CA 94086

Write to them for their current price lists and catalog.

BULLETIN BOARDS

There are bulletin boards all over the country. Most of them allow free access. But a few low life bastards have taken advantage of these boards for criminal and illegal practices. Stolen telephone credit card numbers have been posted on some boards. The owners of the credit cards would then get bills totaling up to thousands of dollars for calls charged to the stolen numbers. There have been cases of insane vandalism where a person would access a board and erase and destroy all of the files. So most of the boards now require some kind of identification and verification before they will give you a password that will allow you unlimited access.

The vast majority of bulletin board operators, or Sysops for system operators, are eager to help you in any way they can. They can be a great help to anyone who is into computers, especially a beginner.

Most of the bulletin boards have hundreds of software programs that can be downloaded to your system. They usually have some documentation for the software that can be downloaded at the same time.

Often there are programs called shareware that are available on the bulletin boards. These are programs that are usually written by a small company or an individual. They encourage you to copy the program and use it. If you find the program helpful or worthwhile, they ask that you send them a nominal fee. For this fee, most of them will register you so that you will automatically receive updates, support and extra documentation.

Besides offering public domain software, most bulletin boards will allow messages to be left on them. It can be just a chatty, gossip type message, or you can list equipment that you want to buy, sell or swap. Some have a corner of the board for bartering.

If you are having a problem with some program, or with your computer, just leave a message for help, and chances are that someone will come up with a solution for you. Bulletin boards and user groups can be a great help for those who are just getting into computers as well as those who have been at it for some time. There is always something new to learn. Most people like to share their discoveries with others.

There are all kinds of bulletin boards. Some specialize in certain areas of interest. There are even some adult X-Rated bulletin boards. Some specialize in computer dating arrangements, and many of them specialize in games.

Many of the commercial software packages are copy protected. Most users dislike copy protected software because they limit backup copies and most are difficult to install and uninstall on a hard disk. But many of the hackers who use the bulletin boards love the copy protection schemes. These schemes are much like a game and a challenge to them. Some of them will spend hours taking a program apart to find the key to the copy protection. And of course it's not much fun if no one knows that you have beaten the scheme. So they post the solutions on the bulletin boards.

Who Operates the Boards

Many of these boards are operated by individuals at their own expense. Some of them are funded by corporations or non-profit organizations. To cover expenses, some boards ask for a nominal registration fee.

There are several magazines that carry descriptions and listings of bulletin boards and user groups. This is a free service of these magazines:

Computer Currents
5720 Hollis St.
Emeryville, CA 94608

Computer Shopper
P. O. Box F
Titusville, FL 32781

MicroTimes Magazine
5951 Canning St.
Oakland, CA 94609

MicroTimes and Computer Currents are published in the local San Francisco Bay area. Check your area for similar magazines.

OTHER REASONS TO HAVE A MODEM

Not only can a modem save you thousands of dollars in software costs, it can also greatly increase the utility, versatility and productivity of your computer.

Banking

There are some banks who will allow you to use your computer and modem to do most of your banking. You would no longer have to go to the bank, find a parking space, then stand in line for half an hour for a simple transaction.

Communication

To become a ham operator, you have to learn the Morse Code and pass a test to receive a license. I never became a ham operator because I could not learn the code. But with a computer you don't have to learn a code or take a test for a license. A person with a modem can call any other computer that has a modem. However, while you won't spend money on ham radio gear, you can run up a very large phone bill.

I know ham operators who would rather communicate on their ham radios than make love. There are many computer owners who feel about the same way about communicating with their modems. To these people a computer with a modem and a good communications program is more precious than the wife, the kids and the family dog.

Incidentally, there are computer programs that a ham operator can use to record and decode incoming code. The computer can also be used to send code much faster than any human operator can.

BUSINESS SAVINGS WITH A MODEM

Modems are absolutely essential to large businesses, but a modem with a good communications program can be utilized to great advantage in almost any business endeavor.

Modems can be used for electronic mail. They can also be used to transfer files and data between various computers that may be located anywhere within the company or even in a distant city. They can be used to access service companies such as Dialog, Source, Compuserve, Dow Jones, MCI Mail, NewsNet and others that provide large databases, up to the minute stock market quotations, business and financial information, news, references and research.

In the business environment there are often many different types of computers. Quite often it is necessary to pass information from one to the other. If one of them happens to be an Apple and the other an IBM compatible, you won't have much luck trying to run the diskette from one on the other. But with the proper software, modems can interface and exchange data with other types of personal computers, minicomputers, and mainframe systems.

BAUD RATES

Modems use the telephone lines which are designed for audio or sound waves, so the modem is limited to sending out and receiving bursts of tones. This severely limits their speed, or baud rate. The baud rate is the number of bits transmitted per second.

Another limitation is the quality of the phone lines. I am sure that you have had phone connections that were very bad, with lots of static, crackling and noise. If you are just conversing with someone it might not make too much difference. But if it caused errors in transmission, or some bits were dropped or scrambled, it could be very important. To overcome this, several error checking protocols such as Xmodem, Kermit and others have been devised. Usually, the same type of protocol must be used by both the sender and receiver.

These error checking protocols do not check every individual bit. That would take too much time. Instead they send a block of data, then the receiving end which knows how many zeros and ones should be in that block, checks the number of bits sent. If they are not all there, or if some of the data is unreadable, then the sender is asked to re-transmit that block.

Some of the early modems used rates as low as 50 baud, or about 5 characters per second. There are some modems today that still operate as low as 300 baud, but the more common rate at the present time is 1200 baud which is 150 characters per second. (Each character is a byte, or eight bits, long.) If you are transmitting or receiving a long file, even 1200 baud seems awfully slow, and if you are connected to a long distance phone, it can also be awfully expensive.

Several American companies are now marketing 2400 baud systems. At the present time the vast majority of modems sold operate at 1200 baud. But the 2400 systems are gaining popularity. They will no doubt be the next standard. The prices started out fairly high, at around $800.00 to $900.00. Many of them still list for similar prices, but you should never have to pay list. There are some that are now being discounted for around $500.00. There are a few Far East 2400 baud clones that are being offered for about half the discount rate. They will be coming down even more.

To communicate at 2400 baud, both the sender and the receiver must be operating at 2400. This is one reason the 2400 has not sold more. If you don't know anyone who has a 2400, then you might think that you shouldn't buy one, but most 2400 baud equipment can also communicate at 1200 baud, or even at 300 baud if necessary.

The 2400 baud will be the next standard. All of the service companies mentioned above will now accept 2400 baud. If you are calling long distance, it can cut down on the amount of time that you are on the line. Since they don't cost that much more than a 1200, it might be best to buy a 2400.

A couple of companies have developed 9600 baud modems. The 9600 baud modems can detect telephone line quality and will slow the transmission speed if there is too much static, interference or other decreased line quality. No doubt there will be several more companies offering 9600 baud modems, or possibly even higher speeds, very soon.

TYPES OF MODEMS

There are two main types of modems, the internal and external. Each type has some advantages and disadvantages.

The internal type is fabricated entirely on a single board that plugs into one of the slots in the computer. The telephone line with a small miniature telephone connector is plugged into the small jack on the board from the back side of the computer. Figure 13-1 shows a half-card internal modem.

If you want to have a phone near your computer, you can add an extension by plugging a Y splitter miniature connector into the modem board. The incoming line would be plugged into one side of the Y and your extension phone in the other side. See Fig. 13-2. The modem will answer the phone only if instructed to do so by your communications software. Of course if you use your modem often enough, you could have a dedicated phone line put in.

One of the advantages of the internal modems is that they are usually less expensive than the external ones. An internal modem plugs into one of the slots inside your computer. It is out of the way and there are no messy wires and expensive cables to clutter up your work area.

A slight disadvantage to the internal is that there are no status indi-

Fig. 13-1. A 1200 baud modem on a half card. (Photo courtesy Everex Systems.)

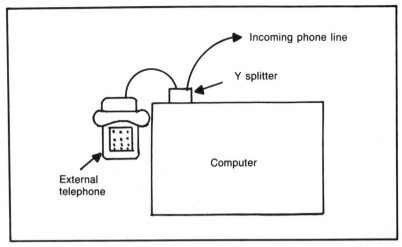

Fig. 13-2. Showing how two phones and the modem can be connected to the one line by using a Y jack.

cator lights to let you know what is happening while you are communicating. Most of the external modems have eight or more status indicator lamps, light emitting diodes (LED's), or liquid crystal displays (LCD's). These will indicate whether you are transmitting (TR) or receiving (RD), whether the phone is "off the hook" (OH) and several other useful bits of information. An internal modem has an on-board speaker and you can hear it dialing and ringing. Most of them do all that they are supposed to do automatically, so you do not have to worry too much.

One of the disadvantages of the external modems is that they cost more than the internal ones because they must have a case and power supply. They also take up desk space and use up one of your wall sockets for power. The external ones also require the use of one of your slots and a board with a serial port. If you don't have a board with an extra serial port it may cost from $50.00 to $100.00 for one. You then need a cable that may cost as much as $50.00 to connect the modem to the computer.

Besides the messy cables and extra power lines, the external uses up valuable desk space. I never seem to have enough space for the books, writing materials and other junk on my desk.

When I bought my Prometheus external modem, I had no choice. I still had my little Morrow computer. It did not have the open architecture of the IBM and there was no way that I could have used an internal modem. But if I were to buy one today, I would buy an internal 2400.

With the proper communications software, most of these intelligent modems can automatically dial or answer calls. If the line is busy, they can re-dial until a connection is made. Some communications software will even let your modem operate your computer to dial or answer calls even when you are not there, or at night when you are asleep and the phone rates are lower.

MODEMS AND THE PHONE COMPANY

When you get your modem it will have a notice that says that it is registered with the FCC and meets their standards. The notice will also tell you that you should call the phone company and give them the FCC registration number that you will find somewhere on the modem. See Fig. 13-3. After you have done this you may plug in your modem.

If at any time your modem causes interference with other telephone users on the line, then you must unplug your unit and have it repaired. You are forbidden to repair it yourself because this would void the FCC registration.

Some telephone companies make an additional monthly charge for a modem and any extra extensions. Modem technology has advanced to the point where there is very little trouble with most modems today. Legally, a person is supposed to follow the rules set down above. I don't know what the penalties are for not reporting your modem connection. But I know a lot of people who have never bothered to tell the phone companies that they have a modem.

STANDARDS

Just as IBM has become the de facto standard for Personal Computers, Hayes has become the standard for modems. An internal Hayes 1200B will cost from $300.00 to $400.00. An external Hayes 1200 will cost from $400.00 to $500.00. There are several clones and compatibles that sell for $100.00 to $200.00 less than the Hayes.

COMMUNICATIONS SOFTWARE

A few years ago communications software for modems was difficult

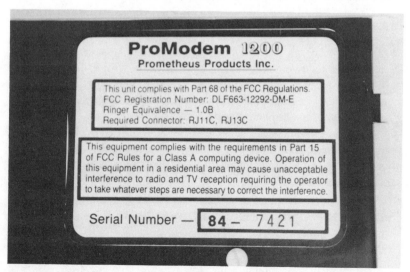

Fig. 13-3. The FCC registration number on the bottom of my Prometheus modem.

to learn and use. Most of it was somewhat less than "user friendly." But with today's technology, more powerful computers, and expanded memories, the software developers have devised some excellent communications software.

One of the newer packages is called RELAY Gold. It was designed primarily for business and corporate use, but it is rather inexpensive. It is menu driven and is very easy to learn and use. At the same time, it is very powerful.

It has a built-in editor that is similar to the IBM mainframe editor. This editor can be used for most simple word processing needs. It has lots of on-screen help and is very simple to learn and use. It also has a built-in programming language that is similar to the IBM mainframe language. It has several other excellent features that make it an outstanding piece of software.

It can communicate with most other communication programs, including many mainframes, but works best when communicating with another RELAY Gold user. The program is not copy protected, but it will check the serial number of any other RELAY Gold that it is communicating with and if the serial numbers are the same it will not let you continue. It lists for $225.00, but is available from several outlets for as low as $133.00.

Of course there are many other communications software packages. If you can get by with a few less features than RELAY Gold has, there are some very good ones that are free from most bulletin boards. Some of the programs such as PC Talk, Qmodem and Procomm ask for a small donation if you find the program helpful. You are under no obligation to pay it, but these people put a lot of time and effort into the development of these programs, so if you use one of them, you should by all means send in a small donation. Otherwise your conscience will bother you.

PARAMETERS

In order for two computers to communicate with each other there are several parameters that must be the same on each end of the line. For instance, if you try to communicate with someone at 1200 baud and they only have a 300 baud modem, it won't work.

There are several other parameters such as the protocol, parity, stop bits, and others, that must be the same or be compatible. Most of the newer software packages make these settings very easy to set or they set them automatically.

BUILD YOUR OWN CABLES AND A-B SWITCH

When I bought my external modem and brought it home one of the first things that I noticed was that I needed a cable for the modem to the computer. Most modems use the RS-232 connector and cable. I checked some of the computer stores and catalogs and found that a cable would cost anywhere from $25.00 up to $50.00. I decided that I could build one for much less money, so I went down and bought a couple of connectors for $3.50 each. I took some wire out of my junk box and built my own in about an hour.

My little Morrow computer only had one serial output port which was used for my printer. When I wanted to use my modem, I had to disconnect the printer and plug in my modem cable. My computer was positioned near the wall and it was very difficult to get behind it. So I decided to buy an A-B switch box that would allow me to switch back and forth from the printer to the modem. I tried several computer stores but wasn't able to find one. I checked through some computer supply catalogs and found several listed at prices ranging from $45.00 to $150.00. I also decided that I could build a less expensive A-B switch box.

An A-B switch requires at least two DB-25S female sockets; one for the printer, and one for the modem. It also requires either another DB-25S for the computer input, or a cable with a DB-25P male plug to plug into the computer. These connectors can be ordered through catalogs for about $3.00 each. It also requires a switch. There are 25 pins in the DB-25 connectors, but a printer or modem will not use more than 8 or 9 of them.

There was a computer swap meet in town so I went down and rummaged through the junk. For $7.00 I could have bought connectors and flat ribbon cable to build a modem cable. But then I found a cable on sale for $10.00. I bought it and also a used cable with a DB-25P connector on one end for $1.50. I also bought a couple of used DB-25S connectors for 50 cents each. I couldn't find a switch that would switch 8 lines so I bought 4 double pole double throw slide switches for 25 cents each.

I mounted the parts in a clear plastic box that had originally been used to pack some electronic components. The box has a hinged lid and is $4'' \times 6'' \times 1''$. It took me about two hours to cut the holes in the box, mount the connectors and switches, and to solder the wires onto the switches and connectors. Instead of the plastic box, I could have used a metal mini box, a wooden cigar box, or even a stiff cardboard box. There is no dangerous power through these cables and connectors so you can use almost anything. Figures 13-4 and 13-5 show my low cost A-B switch box.

If you decide to build a switch box or a printer or modem cable, you should check your computer manual for the output connections. Table 13-1 is the RS-232 recommended standard but not all manufacturers adhere to it.

Again, check your manual to determine just how your computer, printer and modem are wired. Notice that some of the pins are switched. For instance, 6 to 20 and 20 to 6.

If I had gone to a store and bought all new parts for the switch box, it would have cost me between $15.00 and $20.00. My switch box cost only $3.50 and a couple hours of my time. My A-B switch box is not as

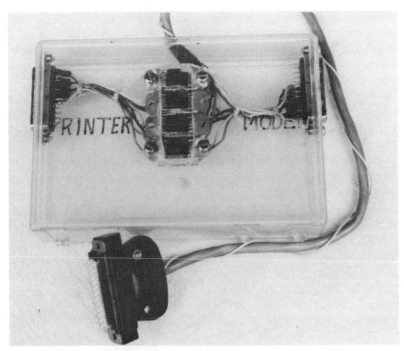

Fig. 13-4. A low cost home built A-B switch box.

pretty as those pictured in the catalogs, but those little electrons going through there don't care doodly about what the box looks like. The main criteria is that it works every bit as well as one costing $45.00, or even $145.00.

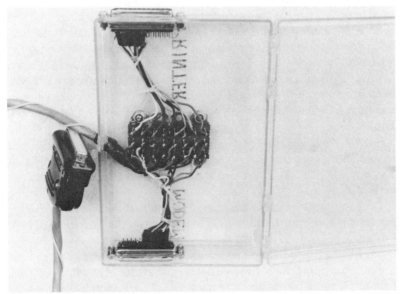

Fig. 13-5. The backside of the switches.

Table 13-1. Standard Serial Cable Wiring for Modems and Printers.

Computer		Printer		Modem	
Pin #	**Function**	**Pin #**	**Function**	**Pin #**	**Function**
1	Chassis gnd.	1	Gnd.	1	Gnd.
2	Transmit data	2	Receive	2	Receive
3	Receive data	3	Transmit	3	Transmit
4	Request to send	5	Clear to send	5	Clear to send
5	Clear to send	4	Request to send	4	Request to send
6	Data set ready	20	Data term. ready	20	Data term. ready
20	Data term. ready	6	Data set ready	6	Data set ready
7	Signal ground	7	Signal ground	7	Signal ground
8	Data carrier det.	8	Data carrier det.	8	Data carrier det.

Later, when I built my IBM PC-XT compatible, I had only one board with a serial output port, so I continued to use my A-B switch box. The IBM system supports two serial ports as COM1 and COM2. (It also supports two parallel ports.) I could have gone down and bought a board with a serial port, but I was a little short of money and my wife was already complaining. She would insist that I leave my credit cards and check book at home every time I went to a computer swap.

Then one day while rummaging through some junk at a computer swap I found a serial port driver board that was made for the early Eagle. I paid $2.00 for it. It works. In fact, it couldn't work any better if I had paid $200.00 for it. I finally retired my switch box, but if I ever run short of slots, I will remove the Eagle serial board and switch back and forth between my printer and modem.

Chapter 14

Troubleshooting

So you finally finished putting it together and you turned it on for the smoke test. Of course you didn't see any smoke. Most of the components in your computer are fairly low power, and low voltage. The only high voltage in your system is in the power supply and it is pretty well enclosed.

Most of the power supplies have short circuit protection. If too much of a load is placed on them, they will drop out and shut down. This is similar to what happens when a circuit breaker is overloaded in your house.

Even if your computer is working perfectly now, it is possible that sooner or later you could have some problems. You can minimize those possibilities by taking good care of your baby.

If you have a hard disk, be very careful in moving or jarring it, especially while it is running. Too much jostling could cause a head crash.

The fan in the power supply should provide all the cooling that is normally needed. But if you have stuffed the computer into a corner and piled things around it which shut off all its air circulation, it could possibly overheat. Heat is an enemy of semiconductors, so try to give the computer plenty of breathing room.

If you did not get a diagnostic disk from your dealer when you bought your system, you might ask him for one. You may be able to buy an IBM diagnostic diskette. The IBM diagnostic program checks the memory, the disk drives, the keyboard, and most of the ICs in the system. There are diagnostic disks for both the XT and the AT. Since your system is compatible, it will test your system also. There may be some ROM tests that might not test properly, but for the most part it provides a thorough test.

The complete test may take a half hour or more and has codes that can indicate about 200 different errors.

INSTRUMENTS AND TOOLS

There are different levels of troubleshooting. A person would need some rather sophisticated and expensive instruments to do a thorough analysis of a system. You would need a good high frequency oscilloscope, a digital analyzer, a logic probe and several other expensive pieces of gear. You would also need a test bench with a power supply, disk drives and a computer with some empty slots, so that you could plug in suspect boards and test them. Figure 14-1 shows a typical bench test set up. Figures 14-2 and 14-3 show some other useful and handy tools.

You would also need a volt-ohm meter, some clip leads, a pair of side cutter dikes, a pair of long nose pliers, various screwdrivers, nutdrivers, a soldering iron and solder, and lots of different size screws and nuts.

You will need plenty of light over the bench, and a flashlight or a small light to light up the dark places in the case.

Most importantly, you will need quite a lot of training and experience.

COMMON PROBLEMS

However, for most of the common problems you won't need all that gear. I have found that a large percentage of my problems are due to

Fig. 14-1. A technician checking out a mother board. He has several sophisticated and expensive instruments that are used for bench testing.

Fig. 14-2. A clip that is useful for holding and inserting integrated circuit chips.

my own stupid errors. Many are caused by not taking the time to read the instructions, or not being able to understand them. Often a problem can be solved by using our eyes, ears, nose and touch.

Eyes. If you look closely, you might see a cable that is not plugged in properly, a board that is not completely seated, a switch that is not set right, or many other obvious things.

Ears. We can use our ears for any unusual sounds. The only sound from your computer should be the noise of your drive motors and the fan in the power supply.

Smell. If you have ever smelled a burned resistor or a capacitor,

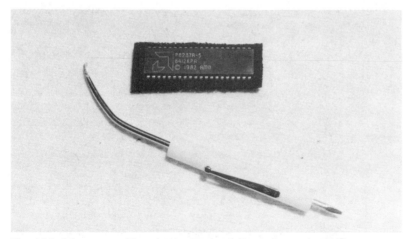

Fig. 14-3. A bent screwdriver that is very handy for prying up large ICs.

you will never forget it. If you smell something very unusual, try to locate where it is coming from. Unfortunately, unless you are highly trained, replacing the part will cost you alot of money, but locating it might save you some of the repairman's $50.00 an hour time.

Touch. If you touch the components and some seem to be unusually hot, it could be the cause of your problem. Except for the insides of your power supply, there should not be any voltage above 12 volts in your computer, so it should be safe to touch the components. However, it is always best to be cautious.

ELECTROSTATIC DISCHARGE (ESD)

Before you touch the components, you should ground yourself and discharge any static voltage that you may have built up by touching the case of the computer. It is possible for a person to build up a charge of 4000 volts or more of electrostatic voltage. If you walk across some carpets and then touch a brass door knob you can sometimes see a spark fly and often get a shock. Most electronic assembly lines have the workers wear a ground strap whenever they are working with any components sensitive to electrostatic discharge.

When I am installing memory chips, or handling other ICs, I often use a clip lead to ground myself. I clip one end to my metal watch band and the other end to the computer case.

RECOMMENDED TOOLS

Here are some tools that you should have around the house, even if you never have any computer problems.

1. Several sizes of screwdrivers. A couple of them should be magnetic for picking up and starting small screws. You can buy magnetic screwdrivers, or you can make one yourself. Just take a strong magnet and rub it on the blade of the screwdriver a few times. Be careful of any magnet around your floppy diskettes. It can erase them.
2. You should also have a small screwdriver with a bent tip that can be used to pry up ICs. Some of the larger ICs are very difficult to remove. IC extractors are not very expensive, so it may be worthwhile to get one.
3. For installing chips, especially the small memory type, a large spring paper clip is ideal for holding them and getting them started, and it will be cheaper than commercially made IC inserters.
4. You should have a few pairs of pliers. You should have at least one pair of long nose pliers.
5. You will need a pair of side cutter dikes for clipping leads of components and cutting wire. You might buy a pair of cutters that also have wire strippers.
6. A soldering iron comes in handy around the house many times. Of course, you'll also need some solder.

7. No home should be without a volt-ohm meter. They can be used to check for the correct wiring in house wall sockets (The wide slot should be ground). They can be used to check switches, wiring continuity in your car, house, stereo, phone lines, etc. You could check for the proper voltages in your computer. There are only four to check for; $+12$ volts, -12 volts, $+5$ volts and -5 volts. You can buy a relatively inexpensive volt-ohm meter at any Radio Shack or other electronic store.
8. You should also have several clip leads. You can buy them at the local Radio Shack or electronic store.
9. You need a flashlight for looking into the dark places inside the computer.

HOW TO FIND THE PROBLEM

1. Diagnostic Software—We mentioned the diagnostic software earlier. By all means, try to get a copy.
2. If it seems to be a problem on the mother board or a plug-in board, look for chips that have the same number. Try swapping them to see if the problem goes away or worsens. If you suspect a board, and you have a spare, or can borrow one, swap it.
3. If you suspect a board, but don't know which one, take the boards out to the barest minimum. Then add them back until the problem develops. **Caution!!** Always turn off the power when plugging in or unplugging a board or cable.
4. Wiggle the boards and cables to see if it is an intermittent problem. Many times a wire can be broken and still make contact until it is moved.
5. Check the ICs and connectors for bent pins. If you have installed memory ICs and get errors, check to make sure that they are seated properly and all the pins are in the sockets.
6. You might also try unplugging a cable or a board and plugging it back in. If the problem could be in a DIP switch, you might try turning it on and off a few times. **Caution!!** Always make a diagram of the wires, cables and switch settings before you disturb them. It is easy to forget how they were plugged in or set before you moved them. You could end up making things worse.
7. If you are having monitor problems, check the switch settings on the mother board. The XT has a DIP switch that must be set for monochrome or color and the AT has a small slide switch. Most monitors also have fuses, so you might check them. Also check the cables for proper connections.
8. Printer problems, especially serial type, are so many that we will not even attempt to list them here. Many printers today have parallel and serial interfaces. The IBM defaults to the parallel system. If at all possible, use the parallel port. There are fewer problems

with parallel ports as compared to serial ports. Most printers have a self test. It may run this test fine, but then completely ignore any efforts to get it to respond to the computer if the cables, parity and baud rate at not properly set.

9. Sometimes the computer will hang up. You may have told it to do something that it could not do. You can usually do a warm reboot of the computer by pressing the Ctrl, Alt and Del keys. Of course, this would wipe out any file in memory that you might have been working on. Occasionally the computer will not respond to a warm boot. You can pound on the keyboard all day long and it will ignore you. In that case, you will have to switch off the main power, let it sit for a few seconds, then power up again.

DOS has several error messages if you try to make the computer do something it can't do. But many of the messages are not very clear. The DOS manual explains some of them, but you might want to get a book that goes into more detail.

If you find the problem is a board, a disk drive, or some component, you might try to find out what it would cost before having it repaired. With the flood of low cost clone hardware that is available, it is often less expensive to scrap a defective part and buy a new one.

Sometimes finding the cause of a problem can be a real headache. Rather than try to find it maybe you should do the next best thing. Just take a couple of aspirins and call a repair shop.

Blue-Icer

Paramount Electronics has developed an automatic diagnostic instrument that can locate a PC or XT problem in just minutes. The 8088 CPU is removed from the "sick" computer. A cable from the Blue-Icer is plugged in and every circuit and component on the mother board is checked. It can save hours and hundreds of dollars in troubleshooting.

Chapter 15

DOS You
Need To Know

Now that you have it all together, you are anxious to turn it on and start computing. If you are familiar with computers, go right ahead, but if you are a beginner, you probably should take a little time to learn a bit about the Disk Operating System (DOS). We can only give a brief explanation of some of the most frequently used commands here.

STARTING UP

Before you can start your computer, you must have a diskette with MS-DOS or PC-DOS on it. Your vendor can probably get a copy for you at a discount price, or you can go to any software outlet and get one for about $60.00 to $75.00. This will also include a large manual that explains the various commands. If you have an XT you can use versions 2.1, 3.0 or higher. If you have an AT you need 3.0 or higher.

You get a manual when you buy a copy of DOS, but the manuals are usually not very clear. I am very proud of the fact that I was able to qualify to become a member of Mensa, but I feel awfully dumb when I try to read and follow the directions in some of the manuals. Many of them make sense only if you already know what they are talking about. It is something like going to a bank for a loan. If you can prove you don't need it, they will give it to you. If you are a beginner you probably should buy a book on MS-DOS or PC-DOS. Several have been written on the subject, which proves that the manuals are difficult to understand. If the manuals were any good, there would be no need for the books!

DOS was developed for IBM by the Microsoft company, so you will often see it called MS-DOS. IBM calls it PC-DOS and there may be some very slight differences in the different versions, but for the most part, PC-DOS and MS-DOS are essentially the same.

There have been several releases since DOS 1.0. Each new release made some improvement or addition to the previous one. At the time of this writing, DOS version 3.2 is the latest, but most PCs and XTs are still using DOS 2.1. DOS 4.0 has been released in some parts of Europe, but it is not expected to be released in this country. Instead it is rumored that DOS 5.0 will be released.

It is called a Disk Operating System because the DOS software resides on disk, rather than in the ROM memory of your computer. It must be loaded into memory each time the computer is turned on and booted up. (Loading DOS into the computer is called "booting up," because the computer "pulls itself up by the bootstraps" from the zero consciousness state of being turned off, to the point where it is able to manipulate input and output, and take commands.) DOS consists of the commands that control the management of data and operations of the computer.

If you have a two disk system, the one on top or the one on the left is usually the A: drive. This is the drive that must be used to boot the system. The diskette must be inserted so that the small square notch is to your left, and the label is up and toward you.

If you have a hard disk, the boot routine can be installed on it and the system can boot automatically when it is turned on. However, unless your dealer has already formatted your hard disk and put the DOS system on it, you will have to boot up from a floppy the first time, then format the hard disk. Refer to your hard disk's manual. The system will always try to boot from drive A: before trying to boot from the hard disk. If there is a diskette there that does not have the boot routine on it, you will get an error message. If you want to leave a diskette in A:, you can leave the door open until after the system boots. If the door or latch is up, the floppy diskette cannot be accessed.

INTERNAL AND EXTERNAL COMMANDS

There are two types of commands, *internal* and *external*. Only the *internal* ones DIR, COPY, DATE, TIME, TYPE, RENAME, BREAK, CHDIR, MKDIR, RMDIR, CLS, ERASE and a few others are loaded into memory. These commands are available at any time after you have booted. The boot diskette can be removed and you can insert another one and still run any of the internal commands. However, if you want to run an *external* command such as CHKDSK to check for the amount of space used by the files on a disk, then you must insert a copy of DOS with the CHKDSK program on it before you can use that command, unless you have a hard disk with CHKDSK on it.

BOOTING UP AND DEFAULT DRIVES

Begin by booting up the computer. Put your DOS system disk in drive A: and turn on the computer and monitor. After a little while, a few messages will flash by, indicating the type of BIOS and DOS that you have. Next, you will probably be asked to enter the date and time. You may enter these if you like, or ignore them by pressing the **Return** key for each of them. Finally, you will be presented with the DOS prompt. It tells you that the computer is ready to receive your commands, and it looks like this:

A>

The "A" tells you that drive A: is the *default drive.* That means that unless otherwise directed, the computer will look for any files it needs on the A: drive. If you have two floppy disks, type in

B:

and press **Return.** The prompt will change to:

B>

which tells you that B: is now the default drive. Change back to drive A: by typing in

A:

and pressing **Return**. Now that the computer is awaiting your command, what will you do? Probably the first thing you want to do is find out what is on the disk.

THE DIRECTORY COMMAND (DIR)

One of the most used of all the commands is the directory. It is difficult to remember just what is on a diskette, and computers are dumb in that you must tell them exactly what to do. If you give a computer a command and you don't type it exactly like the file's name the computer will tell you that it cannot find the file. It will not realize that when you typed "BUGET," you meant "BUDGET."

You can look at a directory in several different ways. If you type:

DIR

and press **Return,** the directory, a list of the files on a disk, will be displayed on the screen. If it is a long directory, it will scroll past on the screen very fast. This is especially true if you have an AT or a turbo system. You can press the **Ctrl** and **S** keys together to stop the scrolling, then hit any key to start it again. You can also use the **Ctrl** and **Scroll Lock** keys to do the same thing. If you use the command:

DIR/P

the computer will display the directory, scrolling up and showing just enough lines to fill one screen, then it will pause and tell you to "Strike a key when ready. . .". If you press any key, you will see the next screenful of the directory.

The command DIR displays quite a lot of information about the files. It tells you whether a file is a .COM file, a .BAS for BASIC, a .TXT for text, or any other extension. It also tells you the number of bytes in the file, and the date and time that it was created or last worked on. This form of the DIR command will also tell you if there are any sub-directories in the directory you are looking at.

DIR/W is a Wide form of DIR that displays the names of the files across the screen. It gets a lot of names in a smaller space because it does not include the number of bytes or the date and time of creation. It also does not list any sub-directories.

Figures 15-1 through 15-3 show the results of using various forms of the directory commands on my DOS disk.

Printing Out Directories and Other Things on the Screen

Sometimes I make a print out of the directory of a diskette and tape it to the outside of the diskette sleeve. You can print the directory by pressing the **Shift** and **PrtSc** (Print Screen) keys while the directory is on the screen. You can also type in DIR, then press **Ctrl PrtSc** or **Ctrl P** before you press **Return**. As soon as you enter the **Ctrl PrtSc** command, everything that is displayed on the screen or is typed from the keyboard is also sent to the printer. The **Ctrl PrtSc** command is a toggle, so to turn it off just press **Ctrl PrtSc** again. The listings used to make Figs. 15-1 through 15-3 were made by pressing **Ctrl PrtSc** before typing the DIR command, so that the command would be printed as well as the directories. **Shift PrtSc** and **Ctrl PrtSc** work for printing anything that is on the screen, not just directories.

FILE NAMES AND WILDCARDS

If you look at the file names, you will see that file names can be no more than eight characters long. If you want to, you may type a period after the first eight and add an *extension* of three more characters. You may use the letters A-Z, either capitals or lower case, the numbers 0-9, and the symbols ! @ # $ % ∧ & ( ) __ { }. You cannot use the characters * + = : ; " , ? / | < > \. Spaces, tabs or any control characters in a file name are also not allowed.

You should try to choose a name that will describe the file as near

```
A:\ >DIR
 Volume in drive A has no label
 Directory of  A:\

TEST      BAT      384    6-28-86   1:30p
ASSIGN    COM     1536    6-28-86   1:30p
BACKUP    COM     6272    6-28-86   1:30p
BASIC     COM    19328    6-28-86   1:30p
BASICA    COM    36480    6-28-86   1:30p
CHKDSK    COM     9856    6-28-86   1:30p
COMMAND   COM    23808    6-28-86   1:30p
COMP      COM     4224    6-28-86   1:30p
DEBUG     COM    15872    6-28-86   1:30p
DISKCOMP  COM     5888    6-28-86   1:30p
DISKCOPY  COM     6272    6-28-86   1:31p
EDLIN     COM     7552    6-28-86   1:31p
FDISK     COM     8192    6-28-86   1:31p
FORMAT    COM    11136    6-28-86   1:31p
GRAFTABL  COM     1280    6-28-86   1:31p
GRAPHICS  COM     3328    6-28-86   1:31p
KEYBFR    COM     3328    6-28-86   1:31p
KEYBGR    COM     3328    6-28-86   1:31p
KEYBIT    COM     3072    6-28-86   1:31p
KEYBSP    COM     3200    6-28-86   1:31p
KEYBUK    COM     3072    6-28-86   1:31p
LABEL     COM     2432    6-28-86   1:31p
MODE      COM     6912    6-28-86   1:31p
MORE      COM      384    6-28-86   1:31p
PRINT     COM     9088    6-28-86   1:31p
RECOVER   COM     4352    6-28-86   1:31p
RESTORE   COM     6016    6-28-86   1:31p
SELECT    COM     3840    6-28-86   1:31p
SYS       COM     4736    6-28-86   1:31p
TREE      COM     3456    6-28-86   1:31p
ATTRIB    EXE     8320    6-28-86   1:31p
FIND      EXE     6528    6-28-86   1:31p
JOIN      EXE     8960    6-28-86   1:31p
REPLACE   EXE    11776    6-28-86   1:31p
SHARE     EXE     8704    6-28-86   1:32p
SORT      EXE     1920    6-28-86   1:32p
SUBST     EXE     9984    6-28-86   1:32p
XCOPY     EXE    11264    6-28-86   1:32p
ANSI      SYS     1664    6-28-86   1:32p
DRIVER    SYS     1152    6-28-86   1:32p
VDISK     SYS     3328    6-28-86   1:32p
        41 File(s)    868352 bytes free
```

Fig. 15-1. The results of the
DIR command on my DOS disk.

```
A:\ >DIR/P

 Volume in drive A has no label
 Directory of  A:\

TEST     BAT      384   6-28-86   1:30p
ASSIGN   COM     1536   6-28-86   1:30p
BACKUP   COM     6272   6-28-86   1:30p
BASIC    COM    19328   6-28-86   1:30p
BASICA   COM    36480   6-28-86   1:30p
CHKDSK   COM     9856   6-28-86   1:30p
COMMAND  COM    23808   6-28-86   1:30p
COMP     COM     4224   6-28-86   1:30p
DEBUG    COM    15872   6-28-86   1:30p
DISKCOMP COM     5888   6-28-86   1:30p
DISKCOPY COM     6272   6-28-86   1:31p
EDLIN    COM     7552   6-28-86   1:31p
FDISK    COM     8192   6-28-86   1:31p
FORMAT   COM    11136   6-28-86   1:31p
GRAFTABL COM     1280   6-28-86   1:31p
GRAPHICS COM     3328   6-28-86   1:31p
KEYBFR   COM     3328   6-28-86   1:31p
KEYBGR   COM     3328   6-28-86   1:31p
KEYBIT   COM     3072   6-28-86   1:31p
KEYBSP   COM     3200   6-28-86   1:31p
KEYBUK   COM     3072   6-28-86   1:31p
LABEL    COM     2432   6-28-86   1:31p
MODE     COM     6912   6-28-86   1:31p
Strike a key when ready . . .
MORE     COM      384   6-28-86   1:31p
PRINT    COM     9088   6-28-86   1:31p
RECOVER  COM     4352   6-28-86   1:31p
RESTORE  COM     6016   6-28-86   1:31p
SELECT   COM     3840   6-28-86   1:31p
SYS      COM     4736   6-28-86   1:31p
TREE     COM     3456   6-28-86   1:31p
ATTRIB   EXE     8320   6-28-86   1:31p
FIND     EXE     6528   6-28-86   1:31p
JOIN     EXE     8960   6-28-86   1:31p
REPLACE  EXE    11776   6-28-86   1:31p
SHARE    EXE     8704   6-28-86   1:32p
SORT     EXE     1920   6-28-86   1:32p
SUBST    EXE     9984   6-28-86   1:32p
XCOPY    EXE    11264   6-28-86   1:32p
ANSI     SYS     1664   6-28-86   1:32p
DRIVER   SYS     1152   6-28-86   1:32p
VDISK    SYS     3328   6-28-86   1:32p
        41 File(s)    868352 bytes free
```

Fig. 15-2. The results of the
DIR/P command on my DOS disk.

```
A:\ >DIR/W

Volume in drive A has no label
Directory of  A:\

ASSIGN   COM      BACKUP   COM     BASIC    COM      BASICA   COM
CHKDSK   COM      COMMAND  COM     COMP     COM      DEBUG    COM
DISKCOMP COM      DISKCOPY COM     EDLIN    COM      FDISK    COM
FORMAT   COM      GRAFTABL COM     GRAPHICS COM      KEYBFR   COM
KEYBGR   COM      KEYBIT   COM     KEYBSP   COM      KEYBUK   COM
LABEL    COM      MODE     COM     MORE     COM      PRINT    COM
RECOVER  COM      RESTORE  COM     SELECT   COM      SYS      COM
TREE     COM      ATTRIB   EXE     FIND     EXE      JOIN     EXE
REPLACE  EXE      SHARE    EXE     SORT     EXE      SUBST    EXE
XCOPY    EXE      ANSI     SYS     DRIVER   SYS      VDISK    SYS
        41 File(s)      868352 bytes free
```

Fig. 15-3. The results of the DIR/W command on my DOS disk.

as possible. If you have a hundred or more files you may forget what is in them unless they have descriptive names. I sometimes use a very short name while working on a file, if I have to load and save it several times. A short name cuts down on the typing strokes. When I have finished it and want to save it, I usually rename it and use all the characters I can plus an extension. This makes the file name more self-explanatory.

There are a few extensions which you should be careful about using. The extensions .COM, .EXE, .SYS, and .BAT have special meanings to DOS, and you should not use them for a file unless they apply. COM and EXE files should be executable programs. SYS files are a special kind of program which runs only when the computer boots up. They set up certain parameters of the DOS environment. BAT files are batch files that will execute a series of DOS commands automatically. A little later, you will learn how to make batch files, and how to use some SYS files.

You may not use the symbols ? or * in a file name, but if you use them as part of a file name in a command such as DIR or COPY, they are called *wildcard* characters. A ? can refer to *any single* character, and a * can refer to *any group* of characters.

Using DIR to Find a File

The DIR command can be used to find a single file, files that are similar, or those that have the same extension. For instance, if your directory had a hundred files in it, and you wanted to look at one named MEDXPNS, you could type

DIR MEDXPNS

it might display

Directory of C: \
MEDXPNS   1792   6-29-86   2:05p
           1 File(s)   20746240   bytes free

If you weren't sure of the name that you had given to the file and typed in DIR MEDEXPEN it would have told you

Directory of C: \ DB
File not found

You could have used the wildcard symbols (? and *), and typed DIR MED?????.* and it would have found any file that began with the letters MED regardless of its extension. Since the computer looks for an exact match for any name that you type in, it is sometimes best to use the wildcards if you are not sure of the exact name.

THE FORMAT COMMAND

You are probably itching to do more than just look at the contents of your disk. For example, you might want to copy some files to another disk, and put the DOS system on another disk so that you can boot up from that disk. However, before you can do anything like this, you need to prepare the blank disk to receive information. This is called formatting.

FORMAT is a very important external command. A new blank disk cannot be used until it is formatted. This command lays out the sectors, tracks and other information needed by the computer to use the diskette. If you have a single drive, put the DOS system diskette with the FORMAT.COM file on it in the drive. To format a diskette, at the A> type the command:

FORMAT B:

The system will display the following message:

Insert new diskette for drive B: and strike any key when ready.

(If you are using DOS 3.2 it will say "Press the Enter key.") After you have put in the blank disk and pressed a key, the following message is displayed on the screen:

Formatting

After about one minute this message is displayed:

Formatting . . . Format complete.
  362496 bytes total disk space,
  362496 bytes available on disk.
Format another (Y/N)?

Unless you want to format another disk, press N. Your disk is now ready to have files copied onto it.

If you had wanted to format a diskette so that the boot-up routine could be installed on it, you would have to give the command:

FORMAT B:/S

This will place some hidden SYS files onto your disk. You could then copy the COMMAND.COM onto it:

COPY COMMAND.COM B:

The new disk in drive B: would now be able to boot up your system. Since the COMMAND.COM and SYS files take up about 40 K of disk space, you might not want to have them on all of your diskettes. After all, you don't usually have to re-boot your computer once it has been started, so just two or three system diskettes will usually be enough. **Note:** Some versions of DOS will automatically put COMMAND.COM onto a disk when you format with the /S option.

It is usually a good idea to have a few formatted blank diskettes on hand. If you need to copy something, and you are in the middle of a file, you can't copy a file unless the new diskette has been formatted. If you stop to format a diskette, whatever you were working on is usually lost, so it is best to have a few that are formatted and ready for use.

If you have a hard disk, and the dealer has not formatted it for you, you will use the FORMAT command to do so. Hard disks are usually known by the computer as drive C:. **However, before a hard disk can be formatted, it must undergo a low-level format. Follow the directions for low-level formatting that came with your hard disk before trying to use FORMAT on your hard disk.**

THE COPY COMMAND

The COPY command is an *internal* command, so it can be used any time the computer is up and running. If the file you want to copy, for instance file ABC, is on A:, you can enter at the A> prompt:

COPY ABC B:

This will copy the file ABC to disk B:. It is possible to use wildcards, the asterisk and question marks, to copy several files at one time. For instance:

COPY *.* B:

would copy all files on A: to B:. We could say:

COPY *.BAS B:

and this would copy all of the BASIC files with the extension .BAS. If we had several WordStar commands and files beginning with WS to be copied, we could say:

COPY WS??????.* B:

and all of the files that began with WS would be copied to B:.

THE DISKCOPY COMMAND

The DISKCOPY command will let you copy an entire diskette onto another diskette whether or not it has been previously formatted. But this copies only entire diskettes. If the target disk has not been previously formatted, it will format as it copies and make an exact duplicate of the original disk. This is the command that you should use to make backup copies of all your programs. The original diskettes should then be stored away in a safe place and the copy should be used for day to day use. Then if the copy happens to become damaged, overwritten, or erased, the original master disk can be used to make another copy.

DISKCOPY is an external command. So you must insert a DOS diskette in a disk drive before using it. To copy a disk, type

DISKCOPY A: B:. (Note the single space between A: and B:)

The computer will display:

Insert source diskette in drive A:
Insert target diskette in drive B:
Strike any key when ready.

It will then tell you how many sectors per track it is copying, either 8 or 9, whether single-sided or double sided, and whether it is formatting while copying. When finished, it will say:

Copy complete. Copy another (Y/N)?

DISKCOPY copies the entire diskette, even if there is only one very short file on the disk. Anything that might happen to be on the target diskette is erased. If you want to copy a file or several files to a diskette then you should use the COPY command, which will never overwrite an existing file unless it has the same name.

DISKCOMP AND FILCOMP

DISKCOMP is a command that causes the computer to compare two diskettes bit by bit. This can verify that a good copy was made with DISKCOPY. Command is DISKCOMP A: B:.

FILCOMP is a command similar to DISKCOMP that can be used to verify that a file was copied correctly, by comparing the two files bit by bit.

FILES WITH THE SAME NAME

You should be aware that if you copy a file to another disk containing a file of the same name, the one on the target diskette will be written over and erased. There are many times when you will want to do this. For instance, if you want to update a file with some current information. If you have a clock/calendar, the files will be dated, so that you can tell which is the current one. However, if you have inadvertently given two different files the same name, it could cause some damage. Before copying, you could RENAME one of them by typing at the prompt:

REN OLDNAME *NEWNAME.*

This command renames file *OLDNAME* to be file *NEWNAME*. It is possible to use wildcards and extensions with REN:

REN *.XYZ *.ABC

will rename all files with extension .XYZ, so that they have the same names, but all of their extensions will be changed to .ABC.

THE TYPE COMMAND

Any text file can be viewed on the screen by using the TYPE command. It will scroll on the screen just like the directory, which is also text. You must type the exact name plus any extension. The three character extensions on files don't show a period when you view the directory, but in order to type out a file that has an extension, you must put a period between the main name and the extension. For instance, the first file listed on the directories printed out above is TEST BAT. In order to view that file you would have to enter:

TYPE TEST.BAT

You can also use **Ctrl S** or **Ctrl Scroll Lock** to stop the file just like stopping a long directory.

By using **Ctrl PrtSc**, you can TYPE out a file and send it to the printer at the same time, similar to the printing of a directory.

Note that I have typed most of the commands in capital letters or upper case. Actually, you may use capital letters or lower case. DOS doesn't care. DOS stores the names of your files in upper case, no matter how you type them in.

THE ERASE OR DEL COMMAND

This is a very useful command, but it should be used with care. It is very easy to erase something that you may not have wanted to. You can use wildcards with ERASE or DEL in the same way that they are used for COPY. You can enter ERASE *.* and wipe out a whole directory, but DOS will ask you "Are you sure (Y/N)?" and will wait for you to confirm it with a Y or N. However, it doesn't ask you if you only erase one file at a time, so be very careful.

If you have the proper software, you can usually recover an erased file. DOS doesn't really erase a file when you tell it to. It erases part of the name of the file in the directory. It is not actually erased until you record something else over it. If you have Norton's utility software programs, you can unerase a file in most cases. It is a very handy piece of software and is relatively inexpensive.

You cannot erase a portion of a file. It is all or none. You can use your word processor, edit the file, and erase portions if you need to, however.

THE MKDIR (MD) COMMAND

If you have a hard disk, this is a very useful command. It makes subdirectories so that your disk is organized. The abbreviated command MD is all that is necessary to invoke the command. For instance, you would want all of your WordStar word processing files in one directory, so you would type:

MD WS

and a WS subdirectory is created. To get to this directory from the main root directory you could type CHDIR WS, or use the abbreviation CD WS. You could then attach sub-directories to this subdirectory if you wanted to by typing:

MD WS \ DCT

To get to this sub-subdirectory, you would have to type CD WS \ DCT. You could add as many sub-directories as you wanted to, but it is easy to lose one, and besides, it is difficult to access them when you have to go through all of them to get to the bottom one.

THE CHDIR (CD) COMMAND

To get to a subdirectory is fairly easy from the main root directory. Just type CD WS. But if you happen to be in the WS subdirectory and want to go to a DB directory, then you must use the PATH symbol the backslash \ like this:

CD \ DB.

To get back to the root directory from a subdirectory, you enter CD \ .

THE RMDIR (RD) COMMAND

If you want to erase a subdirectory, you can use the RMDIR command, for ReMove DIRectory, or you can use just RD. However the directory must be empty.

Say you have a subdirectory named TEMP that you wanted to remove. From the root directory, type CD TEMP to get inside the subdirectory. You must then erase all of the files while in the subdirectory. You can use the wildcard *.* to do this. You cannot remove the directory while within it, so you would go back to the root directory with a CD \ , and then enter:

RD TEMP

This would remove the TEMP subdirectory.

THE TREE COMMAND

The TREE command displays a directory of all of your subdirectories. DOS allows you to create many subdirectories and sub-subdirectories. The main directory is somewhat like the trunk of a tree. The subdirectories are major limbs from the trunk and each limb may have other limbs attached to it. So if you have a good imagination you could imagine that the hierarchy resembles a tree. The tree command displays the names of all the subdirectories on a hard disk.

The tree command scrolls by very fast. Unlike the DIR command, you can't use the /P or the /W options on it. But you can use **Ctrl Scroll Lock** or **Ctrl S** to stop the scrolling.

If you want a print out of your TREE directory, you can type TREE, then **Ctrl PrtSc** before you press **Return**. The listing will be sent to the printer. The actual listing takes five or six lines for each subdirectory, so if you have several, it may take four or five pages.

THE PIPING COMMANDS: SORT AND MORE

When you use the DIR, TREE, or TYPE commands, you can "pipe" their output to the screen through two commands called SORT and MORE.

SORT puts all items in alphabetical order before they go to the screen. MORE outputs items one page at a time.

To use them, simply follow the command by using the piping symbol ¦ and SORT or MORE. Figure 15-4 shows a directory listing using both SORT and MORE. The command to invoke it is DIR¦SORT ¦MORE.

Note: In some versions of DOS you will see two files named %PIPE.$$$ in a directory displayed with SORT and MORE. They are temporary files in which DOS stores information about its sorting operations.

MORE COPY FUNCTIONS

If you want to copy a file from the root directory to a subdirectory WS, enter:

COPY *file name* C: \ WS

To copy a file from a subdirectory to the root directory, enter:

COPY *file name* C: \

If you wanted to copy a file from A: to WS, go to WS subdirectory and enter:

COPY A:*file name*

Or you could go to A: and type

COPY *file name* C:

You could have said COPY file name C: \ WS, but since you were in WS just before you went to A:, that is now the default directory on drive C:. You could specify \ WS just to be sure, though.

If you are in the WS subdirectory and you want to copy a file to the DB subdirectory, enter:

COPY *file name* C: \ DB

The file will be copied to the DB directory.

THE CHKDSK COMMAND

The CHKDSK command, which was mentioned very briefly, is a very useful way of detecting disk glitches before they cause you trouble. It is activated by entering:

```
A:\ > DIR|SORT|MORE


     43 File(s)    866304 bytes free
Directory of  A:\
Volume in drive A has no label
ANSI     SYS    1664   6-28-86   1:32p
ASSIGN   COM    1536   6-28-86   1:30p
ATTRIB   EXE    8320   6-28-86   1:31p
BACKUP   COM    6272   6-28-86   1:30p
BASIC    COM   19328   6-28-86   1:30p
BASICA   COM   36480   6-28-86   1:30p
CHKDSK   COM    9856   6-28-86   1:30p
COMMAND  COM   23808   6-28-86   1:30p
COMP     COM    4224   6-28-86   1:30p
DEBUG    COM   15872   6-28-86   1:30p
DISKCOMP COM    5888   6-28-86   1:30p
DISKCOPY COM    6272   6-28-86   1:31p
DRIVER   SYS    1152   6-28-86   1:32p
EDLIN    COM    7552   6-28-86   1:31p
FDISK    COM    8192   6-28-86   1:31p
FIND     EXE    6528   6-28-86   1:31p
FORMAT   COM   11136   6-28-86   1:31p

--More--

GRAFTABL COM    1280   6-28-86   1:31p
GRAPHICS COM    3328   6-28-86   1:31p
JOIN     EXE    8960   6-28-86   1:31p
KEYBFR   COM    3328   6-28-86   1:31p
KEYBGR   COM    3328   6-28-86   1:31p
KEYBIT   COM    3072   6-28-86   1:31p
KEYBSP   COM    3200   6-28-86   1:31p
KEYBUK   COM    3072   6-28-86   1:31p
LABEL    COM    2432   6-28-86   1:31p
MODE     COM    6912   6-28-86   1:31p
MORE     COM     384   6-28-86   1:31p
PRINT    COM    9088   6-28-86   1:31p
RECOVER  COM    4352   6-28-86   1:31p
REPLACE  EXE   11776   6-28-86   1:31p
RESTORE  COM    6016   6-28-86   1:31p
SELECT   COM    3840   6-28-86   1:31p
SHARE    EXE    8704   6-28-86   1:32p
SORT     EXE    1920   6-28-86   1:32p
SUBST    EXE    9984   6-28-86   1:32p
SYS      COM    4736   6-28-86   1:31p
TEST     BAT     384   6-28-86   1:30p
TREE     COM    3456   6-28-86   1:31p
VDISK    SYS    3328   6-28-86   1:32p
-- More --
XCOPY    EXE   11264   6-28-86   1:32p
```

Fig. 15-4. The results of the MORE and SORT piping commands on a directory of my DOS disk.

CHKDSK *d:*

where the *d:* stands for the drive you want to have checked. It will then check out the disk and report any problems. If you enter:

CHKDSK/S

it will give you more detailed information on the disk. If there are any problems you can enter:

CHKDSK/F

and it will fix up the problem by marking the faulty sectors as bad, so that they will not be used by files. If the sectors are already in use by files, you will probably lose some of the data in those files. This is not so bad for a text file, because you can usually retype the lost words with a word processor. However, if the file is a long complicated program that you don't understand, it is lost forever unless you have a backup copy.

When CHKDSK finds errors, it is often a sign that the disk is going bad. It is often wise to copy whatever you can to a new disk, reformat the faulty disk and use it mainly as a scratch disk for experimenting, or for temporarily storing files that are not too important. If the faulty disk is a hard disk, you can backup as much as you can salvage, reformat the hard disk, and copy everything back. Since this is a very time consuming project, I would advise not doing it unless disk problems started popping up on a regular basis. In that case, it might even be time to have the hard disk looked at by a technician before putting everything back on it.

THE PATH COMMAND

PATH is an internal command that will allow you to tell the computer where to look if it can't find a file in the current directory. For example, you would ordinarily not be able to run a program in the main directory of the hard disk while you were in another directory, say the WS WordStar directory, but if you had previously entered the command:

PATH C: \

then the computer would first search the WS directory, since that was the default directory, then look in the main directory of drive C:.

If you didn't want to have to enter the CD \ WS command every time you wanted to use WordStar, you could set up the path to the WS directory by entering:

PATH \ WS

This would cause the computer to look in the WS directory for any program files it couldn't find in the main directory.

The PATH command is most useful when used in the AUTOEXEC.BAT file, which will be explained a little later.

THE PROMPT COMMAND

You can program the prompt so that when the computer boots up, it says, "Hi there. My name is Hal. What is yours?", or you could write a paragraph of instructions, or several pages if you wanted to. Or you can have it do something that is useful such as display the time and date and the current directory.

IBM calls the strings that can be printed at the prompt meta-strings. They have a code so that a single letter or symbol can represent a complex function. Table 15-1 shows the codes and what they do.

To use the PROMPT command, enter PROMPT, followed by the meta-strings you want in your prompt. For example, to display the current directory with every prompt, enter:

PROMPT $P

Note that the "P" was preceded by the "$" symbol.

As you will see in a few pages, I have a PROMPT command in my AUTOEXEC.BAT file. This automatically sets up my prompt the way I want it. The command in my AUTOEXEC.BAT file is: PROMPT $P $T $D.

If I go to DOS in my WordStar subdirectory, this will be displayed:

C:\WS 8:06:29.38 Fri 7-18-1986>

Note that the time does not change until I press the **Return** key

Table 15-1. Meta-Codes for the PROMPT Command.

Meta-Code	Function or Item Added to Prompt
t	Current time
d	Current date
n	Default drive letter
p	Current directory (of default drive)
v	Version number
g	>
l	<
b		
q	=
h	Backspace
e	Escape
_	new line (carriage return and linefeed)
$	$ (string sign)

again. The time is given in hours, minutes, seconds and hundredths of a second.

You may not want the time and the date at your prompt, but it is almost essential to know what subdirectory you are in. I would recommend that you include it in your AUTOEXEC.BAT file.

You may type in any message that you want. For instance, you might type in the following.

PROMPT $p You have turned me on. Please be gentle with me. $g

It will display the directory name, then the message, and then the " > " symbol.

You can change the message or reprogram the PROMPT as often as you wish, or you can eliminate it by typing PROMPT with nothing following it.

THE CONFIG.SYS FILE

The CONFIG.SYS file is read by DOS during start up. It uses this file to configure certain devices and operations of the computer. If your dealer did not install one, you can make your own configuration very easily. The CONFIG.SYS file usually has only four or five short lines that you type in. There is an example on the next page, the elements of a CONFIG.SYS are:

Break. This command is usually included in the CONFIG.SYS file. It lets you stop a long program by pressing **Ctrl** and **Break** or **Ctrl** and **C.**

Buffers. When DOS is reading or writing information to the disk, it is stored in a block of RAM memory first. Depending on your applications, an improvement in the disk read/write time is possible with a fairly large number of buffers. However, the number of buffers does decrease the amount of available RAM memory. The number of buffers can be any number between 1 and 99. The default number is 2.

Files. This value sets the number of files that can be open at one time. It can be any number between 8 and 99. The default number is 8.

Device. This allows you to install special device drivers. The ANSI.SYS is a driver for the screen and keyboard control. We spoke earlier about the 1.2 Mb floppy disk drive that could be used on the XT or PC. In order to use it, the CONFIG.SYS file has to include a special software driver that comes with the drive.

If you want to see what your CONFIG.SYS file looks like, from the root directory, enter:

TYPE CONFIG.SYS

If it is not what you want, you can easily change it, or write a new one. If it is a long file, you might want to copy it into a word processor, edit it, then copy it back to the main directory. If it is fairly short you can use the COPY CON command to make your CONFIG.SYS file. Enter these lines, following each with **Return.**

```
COPY CON CONFIG.SYS
BREAK = ON
BUFFERS = 30
FILES = 10
DEVICE = ANSI.SYS
^Z
```

The ^Z (**Ctrl Z**) can also be done with function key **F6**. It signifies the end of a file created on the CON or console. This is only a sample CONFIG.SYS file. You may create any configuration you choose. Some software needs certain minimum value for FILES or BUFFERS.

THE AUTOEXEC.BAT FILE

The AUTOEXEC.BAT file is a special case of the batch files mentioned earlier. Batch files (files with the extension .BAT) are small text files that contain a list of DOS commands. When you enter their names at the DOS prompt, the commands inside them are executed one after another as if you had entered them from the keyboard. The AUTOEXEC.BAT file is a special case of the batch file because its commands are automatically executed when the computer first boots up. As soon as the parameters and devices in the CONFIG.SYS file have been set up, the computer looks for a file by the name of AUTOEXEC.BAT. If it exists, the commands within it are executed. If it does not exist, then the commands DATE and TIME are executed. If you make an AUTOEXEC.BAT file, and want to be prompted for the date and time, you must add them to the AUTOEXEC.BAT file. A sample AUTOEXEC.BAT file is shown below:

```
CD \ EGA
EGA
CD \
MODE COM1:1200,n,8,1,p
MODE LPT1: = COM1:
DATE
TIME
VERIFY ON
PROMPT $P $T $D$ G
CLS
SYSLOG I.COM
```

When the computer first boots up, it uses the C: drive as default drive. The AUTOEXEC.BAT file begins by changing to the EGA directory wih the CD \ EGA command. Once there, it executes the EGA program to set up my Enhanced Graphics Adapter. Then it returns to the main directory with the CD \ command. Next, the two MODE commands set up the protocol for my serial port, and redirect all output for my parallel port (LPT1:) to my serial port (COM1:). After that, the DATE and TIME commands are executed. The next command, VERIFY ON, tells the computer to check all data going to the disk drives. The PROMPT command, which was described earlier, changes my prompt from a simple C> to a prompt that tells me the date, the time, and which directory is currently the default directory. CLS clears the screen, and SYSLOG/I.COM activates an excellent shareware utility which keeps track of how you use your computer.

If you want to see what is in your AUTOEXEC.BAT file, enter:

TYPE AUTOEXEC.BAT

This will show you the contents of the file. If you want to change it, you can either edit it with a text editor or word processor, or you can use the command:

COPY CON AUTOEXEC.BAT

to create a new one, in the same way that you created a CONFIG.SYS file earlier.

There are many commands which are most useful when used in the AUTOEXEC.BAT file. These are usually commands that set up the system for your whole computing work session. Such commands include PROMPT, MODE, and PATH.

If you create a new AUTOEXEC.BAT file, you don't have to erase the old one. The new one will replace it. Remember that any file with the same name that is recorded onto the same disk or directory will replace the original file.

BATCH FILES IN GENERAL

The AUTOEXEC.BAT file is probably the best known example of a batch file. Batch files can be a powerful, practical and elegant tool. Many of the newer "user friendly" software packages make use of batch files so that an inexperienced person can use the programs. Many have batch files that can create subdirectories and install their programs on your hard disk. Several programs or files can be linked up to run one after the other. The person would only have to type two or three letters and the whole procedure would be taken over and done by the computer. After all, that is one reason for having a computer, isn't it?

Long programs can be written using just the few batch commands, FOR, IF, GOTO, SHIFT, ECHO, REM and the symbols |, %, and >. Whole books have been written on the subject of batch files. We will show only a few very brief and simple .BAT files.

A batch file will always have the extension .BAT on the end of it. You can check your directory for a listing of them by typing DIR *.BAT. You can look at the program itself with the TYPE command.

A batch file can be created either with the command COPY CON, or with a word processor.

I use simple batch files to get to all of my programs in subdirectories. Here is an example:

WS.BAT
```
c:
cd \ ws
wf.exe
ws.com
```

I can enter WS and this will take me to the WordStar subdirectory, load WordFinder (wf.exe), then load the WordStar program.

CHKDSK is a command that I use quite often, but I hate to have to type six letters to do it. So I have this very short batch file called C.BAT:

CHKDSK.COM

If I enter **c** at the DOS Prompt it will do a disk check for me.

Another command that I use quite often is the CLS command to clear the screen. My little S.BAT file does it with the single letter s:

CLS

There are many little programs like this that can save you time and keystrokes. The fewer keystrokes you have to make, the fewer mistakes.

MASTERING DOS

There are many more DOS commands than the few that we have described here. If you turn out to be a true hacker, you will want to know all of the ins and outs of DOS and batch files to make your life easier. Some hackers spend almost more time setting up slick batch files to make their computers easier to use than they spend actually using them, but there is a certain power rush in knowing that you have organized your system in the most efficient possible manner.

I advise that you buy one of the many available books on DOS, as the manuals leave much to be desired.

Chapter 16

Recommended Software

About four billion dollars worth of software have been written for the IBM PC systems. There are off-the-shelf programs that can do just about anything that you could possibly want. There are certain basic types of programs that everyone should have. We will discuss some of them just briefly.

WORD PROCESSORS

No matter what application you bought your computer for, you will need a word processor.

There is a text editor that is included with the MS-DOS or PC-DOS commands called EDLIN, but it is so crude and hard to learn that very few people ever use it.

There are hundreds of word processor programs available, but the one that has out-sold all of the others is WordStar. Most of the publishing houses, TAB Book Company included, suggest or recommend that manuscripts be submitted to them on diskettes using WordStar.

WordStar is not the easiest program to learn. I had a bit of trouble learning it. But now it has become almost like driving a car. I hardly think about what I am doing. It is quite versatile and quite powerful. It is also fairly small and could be easily used on the early 64 K machines.

WordStar is like a car in another way, like a Ford or Chevy, with no extra chrome and a standard shift. WordStar 2000, Release 2, is like a loaded Cadillac, with everything automatic and all the extra luxuries. It is easy to learn, is very user friendly, has lots of helpful menus and an excellent tutorial on diskette. The whole package requires seven diskettes and requires more than two megabytes of space on a hard disk. Of course you don't have to load the whole program in. There are some functions that you may only use occasionally, such as the tutorial which takes up two diskettes.

WordStar 2000 includes several functions not found in the original WordStar. The amazing thing is that the price is just about the same as that for the original WordStar, which is still among the most sold word processors. A recent ad from a discount software house listed both Word-Star and WordStar 2000 for $249.00 each.

Spelling Checkers

Both versions come with a very good spelling checker, either Spell-Star, or the more popular one, CorrectStar. CorrectStar has a large dictionary, over 300 K. You also have the opportunity to add unusual words and acronyms to a personal dictionary.

There are other stand alone spelling checkers. If you have trouble spelling, then you definitely need some sort of checker. I spell fairly well but I get careless in my typing and I hate to proofread my material. A spelling checker can catch my errors a lot better than I can in proofreading.

A spelling checker is very important to anyone who writes anything at all. If you write a memo or a report that has several spelling errors, no matter how good the report, the spelling errors will detract from it. The ability to spell is not a measure of intelligence, but many people believe that it is and judge a person on this ability.

Other Word Processors

There are many other word processors. Some of them may have features that make them better than WordStar in some respects. Some of them may be less expensive than WordStar.

PC Write is a very good word processor that is found on many bulletin boards as shareware. Everyone is encouraged to copy it and give copies to their friends. If they find the program helpful, the users are asked to send a donation to the writer of the software. The program comes with quite a lot of documentation on the disk. But if you send in a donation of $75.00 they will register your copy, send you more documentation and the source code, and they will send you updates as they become available. You can write to them at:

Quicksoft
219 First N, Suite #224
Seattle, WA 98109

Thesaurus

Quite often when I am writing, I have trouble thinking of just the right word. It is fairly easy to reach for the Roget's Thesaurus and look up the synonyms that I might be able to use, but I often lose my train of thought when I do this. There are several Thesaurus programs that can be loaded into memory and lurk off-stage until you need them. Then, by pressing two or three keys, they pop-up as a *window* on your screen.

WordFinder is such a program. I was rather disappointed with it when it first came out. It didn't have enough synonyms, but they came out with an update shortly after and greatly expanded the number of words. WordFinder is a part of my WordStar WS.Bat file, so it is loaded each time that WordStar is loaded.

If I want a synonym for a word that I have typed, I put the cursor anywhere on that word and press Ctrl and F6. A window pops up with all the common synonyms for that particular word. I can use the arrow keys to move the cursor to whichever word that I want to use. I press return, and it automatically replaces the one in my text.

Whether or not a proper word is used is another gauge by which a memo, a report or any form of writing, is judged. WordFinder is published by:

Writing Consultants
300 Main St.
East Rochester, NY 14445

Writing Style

Another program that is essential to anyone who writes is one that checks the writing style. There are several available. One that I like is called RightWriter.

After you have written a memo or a report, you can use RightWriter to analyze it. It will point out wordy phrases, weak sentences, cliches, redundant phrases, slang, the passive voice and jargon. It counts the number of words in a sentence and alerts you if it is too long and complex. It also analyzes the word length and sentences and determines the grade level the writing is best suited for.

RightWriter has over 2200 rules and a 45,000 word dictionary in its programming that it uses to make its recommendations. Its recommendations are just that. There are times when slang or jargon is appropriate, so you are the final judge as to how your writings should be.

Almost everyone can benefit from this program. If you are an English teacher, you probably don't need it. But most of us are rather sloppy in our writing and usage of the language. This software can help you improve your writing so that it is more concise, clear and more powerful. Its list price is $95.00 and is available from:

Decisionware
2033 Wood St. Suite 218
Sarasota, FL 33577

MODEM SOFTWARE

If you don't have a modem now, I am sure that you will get one eventually. You will need some software in order to use it. One of the better programs is one called Relay Gold. It is very sophisticated and powerful. It can be used for business as well as for personal purposes. It has several functions and features not found in most ordinary communications software. For instance, it can be set to have your modem and computer operate at night unattended. The phone rates are lower at night. It also allows one to encrypt messages, has a fairly sophisticated programming language, and can interface with some mainframe systems. A recent ad priced it at $133.00. It is published by:

VM Personal Computing
41 Kenosia Av.
Danbury, CT 06810

An excellent public domain or shareware communications program is QModem. It will do just about anything that you would ordinarily want to do with a modem. It is available on most bulletin boards, or you can write to:

QModem, c/o John Friel III
715 Walnut St.
Cedar Falls, Iowa 50613

They ask for a $20.00 donation, and that is an excellent bargain.

DISK MANAGEMENT

There are several programs that help you manage and keep track of your files and subdirectories on a hard disk. One of the better and least expensive ones is QuickDos, or QDOS. It can sort your files very quickly, scan the disk and display a map of the directory and subdirectories, copy several files at one time, back up the hard disk, and several other very helpful functions. It is a piece of software that every beginner needs. It can also save time and be helpful to the old pro. The price is $29.95, and it is available from:

Gazelle Systems
230 N. 2475 W.
Provo, UT 84601

MORE HELP

HelpDOS is another piece of software that can be very helpful to the beginner. It can be loaded into memory and information on any of the DOS commands or functions can be called up on the screen at any time. It gives a very brief explanation of the commands. Then, if needed, there is a more detailed description of each of them. The price is $29.95 and is available from:

Help Tech
P.O. Box 50834
Palo Alto, CA 94303

SPEED READING

It is almost impossible to keep up with the technology. I subscribe to about 30 different business and technical magazines. It takes a lot of time to just skim through them. So I bought a speed reading program called simply, *Speed Reading, The Computer Course*.

If you have ever taken a speed reading course, you know that they use several different types of machines to flash words and sentences on a screen. This helps to train your eyes to recognize groups of letters and words instantly. The computer with its sophisticated timing circuits is ideal for this type of training.

The program also takes advantage of the computer's clock and timing capability to measure the time it takes a person to read a page or a certain number of words. Then it tests for retention and makes suggestions for improvement.

Almost everyone can benefit from learning to read faster. The price is $89.00 and it is available from:

BBP
24 Rope Ferry Rd.
Waterford, CT 06386

A Free Speed Reading Course

If you own WordStar, you can devise your own speed reading course. The command Ctrl QW will cause a screen to scroll downward from the beginning of a file to the end with a choice of nine different speeds. The command Ctrl QZ will cause it to scroll backwards from the end of the file back to the beginning. Again, you have the choice of speeds. To practice speed reading, just load a long file and press Ctrl QW. The default speed is 3, which is rather fast. A higher number will slow it down, a lower number will speed it up.

DATABASES

One of the most important uses of a computer is in keeping records.

A good database program is almost essential in order to take advantage of this utility.

A database is usually made up of files. Each file is made up of records and each record may have several fields, and each field may be made up of characters or numeric data. It is similar to the telephone system. The telephone books of a whole state could be considered a database of relational files. A telephone directory of a particular city would be equivalent to one large file. This file would have several records in the form of the name, address and telephone number of each individual. Each of these records are made up of fields which are the name field, the address field and the telephone number field. Each of these fields are made up of data that can be characters or numeric data.

Some of the early database programs were rather difficult to learn and use. But many of them have now expanded and become quite user friendly.

A text oriented database that is easy to use and is quite versatile is AskSam. The funny looking name is an acronym for Access Stored Knowledge via Symbolic Access Method.

Most databases are rather inflexible in the structure of the records and fields. AskSam is quite flexible and allows many simple records to be typed in. It can then sort them or manipulate them for you. It is published by:

Seaside Software
538 Parade Dr.
Corpus Christi, TX 78412

COPY PROTECTION

One of the earliest database programs was dBase II. It is similar to WordStar in that it is one of the most popular and best selling. Like Word-Star 2000, it has also expanded to a very large program called dBase III. It is quite easy to use and has lots of help.

The original dBase II was not copy protected, but Ashton-Tate, the publishers of the software, were almost paranoid in trying to keep anyone from making an illegal copy of their dBASE III and Framework programs.

I can understand their concern about software piracy to some extent. It is stealing no matter how you look at it. However, if they had put copy protection on the early dBase II, it is doubtful that the company would have enjoyed the popularity that it has today. Many people were introduced to the program through pirated copies, and then went out and bought legitimate copies so that they could get the documentation, support, and updates. Ashton-Tate has recently removed its copy protection.

It has been estimated that there are at least two illegal copies of Word-Star in existence for every legal one. When WordStar 2000 was released,

164

it was copy protected, but it was so difficult to install and run that MicroPro removed the copy protection and sent unprotected copies to all registered owners.

There are several different types of copy protection. Some methods place a foreign format in a section of the diskette. Some use embedded codes in the machine language of the program that allows the diskette to be read, but not copied. One scheme used a laser to burn a tiny hole in the diskette. When a copy was made of this diskette, it looked for the hole. If it wasn't there it would refuse to run.

One objection to copy protection is that most of them will not let you make legitimate backup copies of your software. It is very easy to damage or wipe out a master diskette. If you are in a business, this might mean a large loss of data, and at least the loss of the time that it would take to get another copy of the program. Many companies, including Ashton-Tate, are giving the customer a backup diskette. Both the original and the backup have the capability of being copied once, so a copy can be installed on a hard disk. If for some reason you want to take it off the hard disk, you can un-install it back to the original diskette.

It is absolutely essential that you make backups of the data on your hard disks. Being mechanical devices, they can and do go down and take all of your valuable data with them. If you back up your disk regularly, you can save most of it. But since some of the copy protected programs can only be installed and un-installed once, they can be wiped out when you copy them along with your backup.

I recently bought a program through the mails. I didn't realize that it was copy protected until I tried to install it on my hard disk. There was only one copy of the program and it could only be run on a floppy disk. I am quite disappointed in it. I went back and looked at the ad and it did mention, in very small letters, that an unprotected copy could be had for considerably more money. It was my fault for not reading the ad more closely.

Breaking the Protection

Many hackers love copy protection. To them it is a challenge, a dare, a game. Most of the large programs have been un-protected by these people. They gleefully pounce on any new software protection scheme and try to find a way to unprotect it. Many of them then put the unprotect method on bulletin boards. So the software publishers have to go back to the drawing boards and come up with another scheme.

There are software packages that can copy some protected programs. COPY II PC is one of the better known ones. They issue frequent updates to the program to try to keep up with the various protection schemes.

They include a disclaimer with each program that states that the software is to be used only as a tool to make legitimate backup copies of your own software.

The list price is $39.95 and $15.00 for updates. Available from:

Central Point Software
9700 S.W. Capitol Hwy. #100
Portland, OR 97219

There are quite a few programs that COPY II PC cannot copy. So this company also manufactures a plug-in board that will let you copy almost everything. It sells for $95.00.

SPREADSHEETS

Spreadsheet programs are essential to business, and even to the single user. They can be used for budgets, financial planning, taxes, forecast sales, analyze real estate investments, create expense registers, prepare invoices and many other uses.

There are several spreadsheet programs. One of the flashier and better known ones is Lotus 1-2-3. It has some excellent capabilities, but they are very concerned about copy protection. They recently lost out on a large military order because they would not sell unprotected copies.

A spreadsheet program that will do almost everything that Lotus can do is SuperCalc 4. It is not copy protected and was selected by the military over Lotus for that reason.

A recent ad from a discount house offered SuperCalc for $189.00. Lotus was priced at $329.00.

UTILITY PROGRAMS

I would strongly recommend that you buy a copy of a utility software. These are programs that help with disk management, copying, and making other tasks easier and simpler. The Norton Utilities is the best known of this type of program.

One of the most useful of all the Norton Utilities is the Unerase utility, which can recover erased files. When a file is erased, only the directory is changed. The actual data is still on the disk until something else is recorded over it. Quite often a file will be erased accidentally. It is very easy to do. This one utility can be worth the $59.00 price many times over.

BACKUP

We have spoken of the importance of backing up many times. There are several ways of doing it, with hardware and with software. One of the better software programs for backup is FastBack. It formats a diskette while it is copying the files from disk. Formatting slows it down a bit, but if one of its formatted disks is used for the second time to back up your files, it really speeds through it. It also manages to get about 450 K of data on each disk.

Originally, it was copy protected. You had to use the original diskette in order to start the backup. They offered to sell an unprotected copy for $25.00 over the $179.00 price of the protected copy, but you had to sign a statement that you would be bound by the software laws of Louisiana. This state has the strictest laws against software piracy in the country. They have recently announced that they have removed the copy protection. It is published by:

Fifth Generation
7942 Picardy Av. B-350
Baton Rouge, LA 70809

INTEGRATED PACKAGES

There are several software packages that have multifunctions, such as Framework, Symphony, Paradox and others. These programs have the capability of doing basic word processing, spreadsheets, databases, outlining, and other functions. Some of the newer ones and later releases are very powerful and easy to use. They usually cost from $400.00 to $600.00.

PROJECT MANAGEMENT

If you are working on a large project, there are certain events that must happen concurrently, or previously, to putting it all together. In building a large building, there may be a hundred different operations that must be done. The different times when the plumbers, the electricians, the carpenters and all the materials must be on site must be carefully planned. There are several project management software packages such as Harvard Total Project Manager, Milestone, EasyGantt and many others that can be very helpful in planning and running almost any kind of project. Prices may range from $50.00 up to $5000.00.

BASIC

We mentioned earlier that if you buy a clone, you should buy a copy of GW BASIC. Many programs and games are still done with the BASIC language. IBM puts most of their BASIC in ROM, but the GW BASIC is completely disk based, and works on most clones.

SYSTEM LOG

Many people use their computers at home for business purposes. If you do, you are entitled to certain tax deductions, but you must be able to prove to the IRS that it is used for business. One of the best ways to do this is to keep a log. There are several software programs available that will let you use your computer to keep the log.

One of the better packages for this purpose is called Syslog. It is a shareware program and can be found on many bulletin boards.

I have installed it in my autoexec.bat file. Every time my computer is turned on, the Syslog command is run. A message comes up on the screen with the date and time and asks for the name of the individual and then the project. At the end of the session, you must log off and a record is written to a file that includes the name, or initials of the individual, the project worked on and the total time. You can review this record at any time or print it out at the end of the year and show it to the IRS if they question you.

It is a very simple program. All the documentation needed is provided with the program. The developers ask for a registration fee of $25.00 and they will accept checks and credit cards. Of course you don't have to send in the money unless you think it benefits you, and your conscience bothers you, but it is worth much more than $25.00.

They have just sent me a newer version than the one I have used for the last year. This version has password capability and can restrict a person to a particular program. Among several other things, it can monitor a computer and determine the actual time that there is any activity on the keyboard, disk drive or printer. It will allow five minutes of "think" time before it starts keeping track of the idle time. Of course these are optional utilities and you don't have to use them.

This program is ideal for many businesses. Many firms would like to be able to keep track of who is using their computers and the time they spend on them, and what they are doing while running them. They ask for a bit more for business use on a single computer. For multiple machines, they ask for a fee of only $18.00 per computer. If you can't find this program on a local bulletin board, write to:

Apex Resource
23 Christine Ct.
Stormville, NY, 12582

Or you may call them at (914) 221-2611.

Chapter 17

Computer Furniture and Supplies

Now that you have your computer up and running, there will probably come a time when the spouse will insist that you take it off the kitchen table. Spouses can certainly be unreasonable at times.

If you have lots of money you can go to one of the computer furniture stores and buy a computer work station. A desk alone can cost from $200.00 up to $1300.00. The chair for the desk is usually extra for $50.00 up to $250.00.

If there is no store near you, there are several companies who send out computer supply catalogs. I seem to get one in the mail about every other day. The prices for the supplies in these catalogs are usually about twice what you would have to pay anywhere else.

Most of these catalogs will have a section on computer furniture such as desks, chairs, file cabinets, protective enclosures for your floppy diskettes, stands for your printer, sound enclosures for your printer, and even dust covers for your computer and peripherals.

Computer furniture is big business. A while back, a business magazine had an article about some high tech companies here in Silicon Valley. It named a couple of companies who had raised several million dollars to go into the business of manufacturing disk drives. At about the same time a young man borrowed $20,000.00 and bought some woodworking tools. Six months later the two companies who had raised millions to go into high tech manufacturing were belly up and bankrupt. The young man who had borrowed the money to buy the woodworking tools was selling as much computer furniture as he could make. He was well on his way to becoming a millionaire.

The way I figure it, if you had lots of money, you wouldn't be building a clone. You would probably go out and buy a genuine IBM and not care diddly that it cost two or three times as much. If you had that much money you probably wouldn't care how much the computer furniture cost either.

It's much more likely that you're like me. You want to save all you can. Besides, if you can save a bit on furniture, you can probably buy an extra board or piece of software for your computer.

MY COMPUTER TABLE

My computer table is made from an old treadle Singer sewing machine. The guts of the machine were thrown away years ago. The top was good and the iron grillwork legs were strong and steady so it made a good work table for the garage. I had no desk or table when I got my first computer and my wife wouldn't let me use the kitchen table at all. So I dug out the old sewing machine table and re-worked it a bit.

With the leafs folded out, it was long enough, but it was rather narrow. It was also a bit high. So I bought a piece of plywood 14 inches wide and four feet long. I screwed it to the underside of the sewing machine table and then braced it. It is just right for my keyboard and it gives me plenty of space on each side for papers, reference books and junk. I don't think I could have bought a better table.

PRINTER TABLE AND STAND

I also built a plywood table for my printer. I made it the same height as the sewing machine table. It gives me lots of working area.

There are several companies that make stands for the printer to sit on so that the continuous sheet computer paper can be stored underneath. It is a very good idea, but they cost anywhere from $20.00 to $50.00. I took four bricks and put two under each side of my printer. They work great.

Like most printers, mine is a bit loud and can be disconcerting. It is possible to buy enclosures that are lined with foam rubber to deaden the sound. They can cost from $200.00 to $500.00, so I took some foam rubber and placed it between the bricks and the printer. It isn't as good as a $500.00 enclosure, but it cut the noise down by about half. If I had the time I could buy about $20.00 worth of plywood and make a good enclosure. But the noise isn't all that bad.

FILING CABINETS AND DESK

I needed a filing cabinet so I went down to a store that deals in used office furniture. I bought a four drawer cabinet for $60.00 and a chair and desk for $100.00. The cabinet and the desk had some scratches and dents, but the drawers work fine and that is what is most important to me. The chair needs new casters. One of these days I will get the time to replace them.

There are several unfinished furniture stores in the area. I could have gone to one of them and bought a fairly good desk and table for my computer at a fairly reasonable price.

Of course if you are the least bit handy at such things you can go down and buy the lumber and make your own tables and desks. Even if you are not very handy and don't have many tools, you can buy a couple of sawhorses that clamp together then buy a sheet of plywood to lay over them. You might even take one of your wife's table cloths and cover the plywood. If she objects, you can buy an oilcloth of your very own for a very nominal sum.

LIGHTING

My kids have grown up and left home, so I converted a small bedroom into my computer room. I am fortunate in that it has a large window that lets in plenty of light and fresh air, but when I am working at night, I have a pole lamp off to one side of my computer so that I have no glare. It has three lamps on it but I only use two of them. I have installed a 75 watt incandescent bulb as one of the lamps, in the other I bought a screw-in type fluorescent. The mixture of these two lights seem to work very well for me.

FILING CASES FOR DISKETTES

If you are like me, there will probably come a time when you have more diskettes than you know what to do with. It is important that the diskettes be cared for properly. They should be protected from dirt and dust, any strong magnetic fields, from coffee, from cigarettes, smoke and ashes, from bending or rough handling. You should never touch the diskette through the slotted opening. A greasy fingerprint could wipe out some of your data.

Several companies have plastic, wooden or metal enclosures that can sit on the desk and hold from 10 to 50 diskettes. They are quite handy and it is easy to organize your software so that it is easy to find. They may cost from $10.00 up to $50.00.

I bought one that holds 50 diskettes (see Fig. 17-1), but it was filled to overflowing in a very short time. I have my filing cabinet at the end of my computer table. So I used the third drawer for filing my floppy diskettes. I set up two rows across the front of the drawer with about 100 diskettes in each row. It is very handy. I have only to pull the drawer out, flip through the diskettes until I find what I want, then close it. It frees up my desk by quite a bit and saves me time in trying to locate the various programs that I might need. See Fig. 17-2.

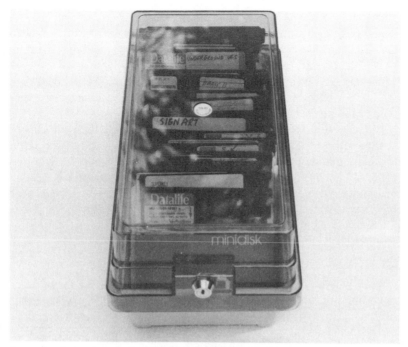

Fig. 17-1. A plastic case for holding floppies. It can hold 50.

Fig. 17-2. The front portion of one of my filing cabinet drawers can store over 200 floppies.

172

Fig. 17-3. A plastic Ziploc sandwich bag is ideal for storing your masters and important diskettes. Each bag will hold about five diskettes and protect them from dirt, dust and moisture.

Ziploc Plastic Bags

As we said earlier, we should be especially careful with our masters. I found that the Ziploc plastic sandwich bags made by Dow were just the right size for a diskette. In fact, you can put about five diskettes in one, then zip it closed. They will be protected from dirt and dust and even moisture. They are ideal for storing your diskettes. See Fig. 17-3.

Occasionally, you might have to mail a diskette. There are stiff cardboard mailers available, but to give it more protection, you can place the diskette inside of a Ziploc bag, then inside the mailer.

I wrote to Dow and suggested that they use some of their vast advertising budget to let people know about their ideal diskette protectors, but a manager wrote back after several weeks and politely informed me in so many words that they were in the food business. Their bags were made for sandwiches and they had no interest in promoting them for other purposes. I sure wonder how they got to be such a big company with managers like that one.

Chapter 18

Manuals
and Documents

Any time you buy a piece of software or hardware, you should get some kind of documentation or an instruction manual with it. The kind of documentation that you receive will depend on the type of package and the company. See Fig. 18-1. The documentation provided by some of the clones is little more than a few photocopied, type-written pages of pidgin English (Fig. 18-2). The WordStar 2000 program comes with six different spiral bound manuals.

The word "document" is derived from the Latin "docere" which means to teach. One dictionary definition says that a document is any written item such as a book, article or letter, especially of a factual or informative nature.

The word "manual" is derived from the Latin meaning hand. A manual is usually a small handbook, especially one giving information or instructions.

The definitions above tell you what manuals and documents should do; teach, instruct and inform you. However, many of them fail miserably in their attempts to do this. Talk to anyone, novice or pro, and chances are that he or she can give you several horror stories about their experiences with manuals and documentation, or rather the lack of it.

When I bought my first computer, I eagerly set it up and tried to load a simple BASIC program that came with the system. I tried for quite a while, then finally got out the 400 page manual. About half way through the manual, I found an example of a program being loaded. I noticed

Fig. 18-1. Some of the various types of manuals and documentation.

that it had quotation marks at the beginning of the name of the program. I went back and put the quotation marks in front of the name and it loaded immediately. Nowhere in the manual did it say that you had to use quotation marks to load a program. I have since gone through several other BASIC manuals and none of them mention this absolute requirement. The IBM BASIC manual does not even list quotations in the index. But BASICA and GW BASIC configure the function keys for several operations. Pressing F3 causes the Load command to be invoked with the quotation marks automatically inserted. You also need quotation marks to Save a BASIC file to disk, so F4 invokes the Save command with automatic quotation marks.

---

a feature. In normal mode. The processor operates at 4.77 MHz. This frequency, which is derived from a 14.318 MHz crystal. When you change mode to ultra mode. will give you an increase of almost 40% in speed of program execution. at the time, the pro-cessor operates at 6.67 MHz. it is from 20 MHz crystal. is divided by 3 for the processor clock, and by 4 to obtain the 3.58 MHz color burts signal required for color televisions.

At the 4.77 MHz clock rate, the 8088 bus cycles are tour, clocks of 210 ns, or 840 ns. I/O cycles take five 210 ns clocks or 1.05 microsecnds. at the 6.67 MHz clock rate. the bus cycles are four, clocks of 150 ns, or 600 ns. I/O cycles take five 150 ns or 750 ns.

Fig. 18-2. A couple of paragraphs from a manual for a clone mother board.

Recently, I was able to convince my boss that I could save a lot of time if the company would buy a serial print buffer for the computer I use at work. When the buffer arrived, I tried for quite a while to get it to operate. A small manual came with it. The buffer had several switches and jumpers that had to be set to configure it to the printer or plotter being used and the computer driving it. I went through the manual several times and made sure that I had set all the switches and jumpers according to the instructions. I finally gave up and called the small manufacturer long distance. They gave me some instructions that were a bit different from the manual. It still didn't work. We finally brought in some test gear and determined that it was a defective unit. We got a new unit and configured it according to the instructions in the manual and it didn't work. There was a brief schematic in the back of the manual. We re-set the switches and jumpers according to the schematic and it worked fine. We found out later that there were two other units in another department that had been sitting on the shelf because no one could get them to work. They configured them the same as mine and they are now working as they should.

My boss was not too happy. I wasted more time in getting the buffer to work than I will probably ever save by using it. But he shouldn't have blamed me. He should have blamed the company and their poor quality control and their cheap manual. I wrote them a nasty letter.

I can sympathize to some extent with the people who write manuals and reference documents. The software and hardware that the manuals are written for will be used by a diverse group of people all the way from novices to experts. The writer must try to satisfy the needs of each of them. A manual should not be so simple that it will turn off the expert, nor so technical that the novice cannot understand it, but many manual writers can't seem to bring themselves down to the novice level. They often use unfamiliar jargon and computerese that frightens and discourages new users.

Another factor that writers must consider is that many people do not read very well, or they don't like to read. Instructions should be simple and as brief as possible. If a manual is well written, you should be able to take any person off the street, sit them down and have them follow the directions with a minimum of help. Alas, very few are this good.

WHAT CAN BE DONE

These are some partial solutions.

Company Training

Many large companies have set up training departments to give their workers hands-on training. It takes a fairly large amount of money to install computers and hire teachers who can devise classes and instructions for the most popular programs.

Computer Store Training

Several computer stores here in the San Francisco Bay area have developed classes for the various software programs. If you buy a computer or software package from them, they may give you the class free. For others they charge only a nominal fee. The more people they can train, the more likely is the chance that they will buy a computer.

Community Colleges

Here in Silicon Valley, there are six community colleges within a ten mile radius. There are also three large universities in the same area. All of these schools offer extensive computer classes. Many of them offer these classes at night so that the person would not have to miss work.

Most other community colleges, and some high schools, throughout the country offer similar type classes.

On-Disk Tutorials

Many of the larger software packages, like WordStar, Lotus 1-2-3, dBase III, and others, come with on-disk tutorials. Many of the programs offer on-screen help that can be called up while you are running the program. Of course these help messages require memory which is one reason they were not offered in the early days. At one time, 64 K was alot of memory. Now 640 K is the de facto standard, so we can afford to use some of it to make the programs "user friendly."

Vendor Support

Many of the larger software companies maintain a large staff of people to answer the questions of their customers and give them help when they have problems. Usually when you call one of these companies, they will ask you for your registration number or serial number of the software package. This is to make sure that you are a legal owner of the software. There are some people who make illegal copies of software and then call up the publishers and ask them for help in order to use it. This is very foolish.

Many people complain about the high cost of software. The support that the companies offer is one reason for the cost, but in many cases, if they wrote better manuals, they wouldn't need to provide so much support.

Keyboard Overlays

WordStar 2000 and some of the other large packages now come with a keyboard overlay that has the most frequently used commands. WordStar also has ten of the Function keys pre-programmed for the most common commands. If you don't like the way they are programmed, the install program lets you program them to suit your own needs.

There are several private companies who are manufacturing plastic overlays for all of the more popular software programs. Here are the names and addresses of a couple of the companies:

Systems Management Associates
3325 Executive Dr.
Raleigh, NC 27609

Inmac Computer Supply Catalog
2465 Augustine Dr.
Santa Clara, CA 95054

The Systems Management Associates charge $14.95 for each of their overlays, the Inmac Catalog lists a price of $19.95 each, but these overlays can be worth much more than that by saving time in learning and using the programs.

Seminars

I am almost inundated with junk mail for seminars. Most of them cost from $500.00 to $900.00 for a one or two day seminar. I am very proud of the fact that I was able to pass the test to become a member of Mensa, but I am sure that I could not learn $500.00 worth of information in one day's time.

Evidently companies and some individuals are able to write the cost of the seminars off their taxes, or otherwise be able to afford them. The money these people spend for junk mail alone means that they must be getting thousands of students. If you can get your company to pay for your attendance, or if you have lots of money, then by all means you should attend them.

Books

Every computer store has a rack full of computer books. They will usually have several books on the large software packages. If the manuals that come with the software were any good, then there would be little need for all of these books.

Even if the manuals were perfect, some people would still want a different book to augment their manuals. A lot of the books are also bought by people who have made illegal copies of the software and therefore do not have original manuals.

CONFLICT OF INTEREST

In a recent column in the Computer Currents Magazine (Aug. 12-25, 1986), Bernie Zilbergeld lamented the poor state of manuals and documentation. He even went so far as to intimate that perhaps some software companies are deliberately publishing inferior manuals. He pointed out

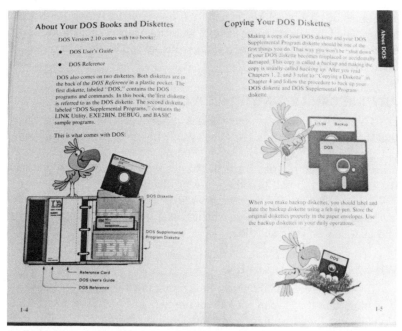

Fig. 18-3. A couple of pages from the Disk Operating System User's Guide showing the juvenile cartoons.

that Microsoft publishes and sells MS-DOS and MS Word. Both of these manuals are published by Microsoft Press, which also publishes and sells a book called Running MS-DOS and another called Getting Started With Microsoft Word. He says that the two latter books are much better than the manuals that are issued with the software.

I am sure that a company as large as Microsoft would not do this deliberately. As we said earlier, it is almost impossible to write a book that would satisfy everyone. It is likely that Microsoft is trying to fill in the gaps and reach those people who are not comfortable with the original manuals.

Microsoft publishes a small manual for IBM called the Disk Operating System User's Guide. It explains the most used DOS commands very well. It is a booklet that would help any person who was just getting started. But it was obviously written for young children. It has several juvenile cartoons throughout the book (See Fig. 18-3). Many adults might be ashamed to be caught reading it. Aside from that, it can be a great help for the novice.

COPYRIGHT PROTECTION

At the office where I work, several people have access to the two computers. All of them need to use the manuals from time to time. If I am not careful, someone will forget to return the manual, or somehow it will disappear. I would like to be able to copy all of the manuals and put copies by each machine, but there are very strict copyright laws. I have violated the laws to some extent. There are usually small quick reference cards with each software package. I have copied those and placed them by the computers.

ANYONE CAN LEARN TO USE A COMPUTER

There are still many people who are afraid of computers. Many think that they are so complicated that they would never be able to learn them, but that isn't so. Anyone can learn. You may not ever become a great programmer, but you can learn the basics very easily, and as you use the computer, you will become more proficient.

Again, users groups can be a great help if you have problems. There is almost always someone there who has experienced the same problems and can answer your questions.

WHY YOU SHOULD LEARN

If you have used a computer, then you know the value of them and how important they are to our way of life today. If you have no saleable skill already, then I would suggest you learn computers. In the first five years since the introduction of the IBM PC, they have sold three million units. There are probably almost as many clones in use. There is no question that the personal computer is here to stay.

If you don't have a good job already, if you are out there competing for the few available good jobs, then you need an edge. Learning all you can about computers can help give you that edge.

Computers can not only help you earn a good living, they can be exciting and fun. You can't say that about too many jobs.

Chapter 19

Computer Swaps and Shows

Computer swaps and shows are some of the best places to find great deals.

LOCAL SWAPS

We have mentioned the local swaps several times. Here in the San Francisco Bay area we have one almost every weekend. You would think people would get tired of them, but every one of them is so crowded that there is a danger of being trampled.

There are usually a lot of kids at these swaps. One small show gave a discount for kids. They had a large sign at the entrance that said "Adults $6.00, Children $3.00." There were kids everywhere playing games on the computers. It was difficult to get near a booth. One disgruntled person went out to the sign with a large marking pen and changed it to read, "Children $30.00."

MAJOR SHOWS

There are major shows and exhibits in San Francisco four or five times each year. There are also major shows in Los Angeles, Dallas, Atlanta, Boston, New York and other large cities several times each year.

COMDEX

The world's largest Computer Dealer Exposition (COMDEX) is held in Las Vegas each fall. There are usually over 1200 exhibitors and more than 80,000 visitors. I attended the show last fall. It was quite a spectacle.

Why Las Vegas Instead of San Jose

It may seem strange that Las Vegas is chosen to host a computer show. It is the entertainment capital of the world, while Silicon Valley is the high technology capital of the world so you might think that COMDEX should be held in San Jose, but there are several good reasons why San Jose was not chosen. One reason is that San Jose could not furnish hotel rooms and exhibitor floor space for a show like this.

Las Vegas was little more than a wide place in the road in the late 1940's when mobster Bugsy Siegel opened the first legalized gambling casino there. At that time the principal inhabitants of the place were jack rabbits and rattlesnakes. Las Vegas today has over 600,000 permanent residents and about that many visitors per day. Or at least it seems like that many. They have plenty of hotel rooms and other services for almost any number of visitors.

Las Vegas has also gone all out to attract conventions. They have built a convention center that has over a million square feet of exhibit space and meeting rooms. Even this immense convention center was not enough space to display all of the products that were exhibited this last year. Additional exhibit areas were set up in four other large hotels. Free shuttle buses ran continuously between the hotels and the convention center.

If you compare Las Vegas and San Jose, you can see why no one in their right mind would choose San Jose. Las Vegas is open 24 hours a day. San Jose rolls up the sidewalks at 8 p.m. (or 7 p.m. during Daylight Saving Time). If a bartender in San Jose sells a person a drink one minute after 2 p.m. he could lose his license and receive a sentence just slightly less than that handed out to mass murderers. I am not sure why the State of California is so interested in what time a person buys a drink. I think it must be because they want to be sure the person goes home and gets a few hours sleep before he goes to work the next day. Nevada doesn't care what time you drink. And you won't find a clock in any of the casinos.

So if you consider the bright neon lights, the gambling and the half-naked show girls of Las Vegas, you can see why 80,000 businessmen would use almost any excuse to go to COMDEX. If the show was held in San Jose, it probably wouldn't draw 800 businessmen.

Tax Deductible

Most of the 80,000 visitors, and the exhibitors, at the last show will claim the expenses of their trip as a legitimate tax deduction. If they can have a bit of entertainment in the evening, that should make no difference to the IRS. Unless they try to claim their losses at the gambling tables as a business deduction.

Overwhelming

As we said earlier, there were more than 1200 exhibits. It was absolutely overwhelming. In three days time, I was not able to visit all of the booths and talk to many of the exhibitors. There were also several conferences that I was unable to attend. Some people have complained that the show has become too big, but I don't expect it to change. In fact, I have little doubt that the next show will be even larger. There will be something for everyone. After all, you don't have to visit the booths that don't interest you. When you register, they give you a 385 page program and exhibit guide that lists and describes all of the exhibits, and has maps of where they are located. In addition, about 100,000 copies of COMDEX SHOW DAILY are published and distributed every day. This is a tabloid type paper with about 150 pages of descriptions and ads for the exhibited products. It also has maps and lists all of the booths.

Playing With the Big Boys

There were also a large number of the small companies who were displaying their PC-AT and PC-XT clones at the show. These small companies, many of them just importers, have gained a bit of respectability and regard by displaying their wares alongside the big boys. The big difference between the smaller companies and the larger ones is that they offer more for your dollar. You can buy any part or component from them and assemble your own.

We can't possibly list all new software and equipment at those 1200 booths. There were many, many new products that were very interesting.

SPEC SHEETS AND OTHER LITERATURE

Almost every booth at these shows have several pieces of literature to pass out. Printers must make a fortune off these shows. I carried a large bag with a shoulder strap, but even that got very heavy after making the rounds for a few hours. I saw a few people who brought small two wheel shopping carts to lug their literature around. One person even had a card board box mounted on a two wheeled cart. The box was about the size of a filing cabinet drawer and he had several file folders in the box. When he picked up a piece of literature he filed it in the proper category. How I envy people who are that well organized.

AN ANNUAL OCCASION

All in all, it was a great show, exciting and informative. If you were unable to go last year, I am sorry for you, but the show will be held there again next Fall. I would suggest that you start right now and try to think up a good excuse that would allow you to attend the show and be able to write it off your taxes. I just hope they don't change the tax laws before the next show.

Appendix

Free Magazines

There are hundreds of free magazines that are available if you can qualify. In most cases, the subscription price of a magazine does not even cover the cost of postage to mail it. The only way that they can survive is by selling ads, so many trade magazines no longer charge a subscription price. They will ask you to fill out a questionnaire to determine if you qualify before they will send it to you. Most people can qualify.

Most of these magazines are aimed at a particular group of people in industry or manufacturing. In particular, they would like to influence the purchasing agents in the large companies to buy their advertiser's products. They know that there are only a very limited number of purchasing agents so it would not be worthwhile to print a large magazine for them only. The publishers and the advertisers know that they need a large number of readers in order to make the product known and to sell it, so to have a large circulation they will accept almost anyone who has any influence at all in buying, specifying, or using the products that they advertise. The more names on the circulation list that the publishers can show to the advertisers, the more they can charge for the ads, so they need you.

Since there are so many of these magazines, most of them have looked for a specialized niche and concentrate on that. For instance, Quality Magazine specializes on manufacturing quality, quality assurance, and inspection techniques. Electronic Design has articles and ads that would interest the design engineer.

The magazines have excellent articles that are helpful and informative. Most are written by professional engineers or people who are actually involved in the particular field. They know what they are talking about.

The computer is used more and more in the manufacturing machine shops, on the assembly line and in the offices. It is almost impossible to keep up with the latest technology. These magazines help to a great extent.

Even if you are not involved in manufacturing or industry, there are many articles in these magazines that I am sure would interest you. We cannot list all that are available, so we are going to list just a few of them that deal primarily with computer subjects.

If you would like a free subscription, write to any of the following publishers and ask for a QUALIFICATION FORM.

PC WEEK
One Park Av.
New York, NY 10016

This tabloid format magazine is published by the Ziff-Davis Company, the same company that publishes PC MAGAZINE. This magazine is published weekly and has excellent articles on computers and peripherals. It is free, but they say they have been inundated with free subscription requests. They are trying to honor all who qualify. If you don't qualify, you may send a paid subscription of $120.00 per year.

MICROTIMES
5951 Canning St.
Oakland, CA 94609

This tabloid format magazine is published monthly. It has very good articles on computers, new products and reviews. It is distributed free to computer stores and shopping centers in California. They will send it to your house for $12.00 per year. A great bargain.

COMPUTER SYSTEMS NEWS
600 Community Dr.
Manhasset, NY 11030

This weekly tabloid format magazine is aimed more at corporate officers, but it has some excellent articles on new products and business trends.

INFORMATION WEEK
600 Community Dr.
Manhasset, NY 11030

Published by the same company as Computer System News, this magazine has very good articles on the computer industry and products.

MISWEEK
7 East 12th St.
New York, NY 10003

This is also a weekly tabloid format magazine that has articles aimed at the information systems portion of the business world. It has articles and ads that are similar to those in the Computer Systems News.

QUALITY
Hitchcock Building,
Wheaton, IL 60188

Articles on testing, inspection, computers, and new products are found in this magazine.

COMPUTER CURRENTS
5720 Hollis St.
Emeryville, CA 94608

Published every two weeks, this magazine has articles on computers, new products and reviews. It is distributed free in many shopping areas and computer stores in California. They will send free copies to your home or business if you qualify.

COMPUTER DESIGN
119 Russell St.
Littleton, MA 01460

Published every two weeks, Computer Design has articles on computer systems, technology, design and products.

COMPUTER PRODUCTS
P.O. Box 14000
Dover, NJ 07801

This is a magazine that is limited to ads.

SYSTEMS & SOFTWARE
10 Mulholland Dr.
Hasbrouck Heights, NJ 07604

This magazine is published by the Hayden Publishing Co., the same people who publish PERSONAL COMPUTING. It has advanced articles on systems and software.

DATAMATION
875 Third Av.
New York, NY 10022

Published twice a month by a division of the Dun and Bradstreet Co.,
Datamation has articles on data processing and computers in industry.

DIGITAL REVIEW
One Park Av.
New York, NY 10016

This is published by Ziff-Davis Company who also publish PC Magazine and PC WEEK. It is devoted primarily to the DEC computer systems, although it publishes articles of interest to all computer users.

DIGITAL DESIGN
P.O. Box 8
Winchester, MA 01890

This magazine publishes articles on Computer Aided Design (CAD),
Computer Aided Engineering (CAE), graphics, and other design and engineering functions.

DESIGN NEWS
270 St. Paul St.
Denver, CO 80206

This is published by CAHNERS Publishing Company who publish
32 different specialized magazines. Design News is published twice a
month and has many short news type articles on new products and technology.

ROBOTICS ENGINEERING
174 Concord St.
Peterborough, NH 03458

Robots have taken over many of the repetitive type jobs in factories
and industry. They are our best hope in competing with the low-cost labor that has drawn so much of our manufacturing to overseas plants.
Since robots are computer controlled, they go hand in hand.

ROBOTICS WORLD
P.O. Box 420495
Atlanta, GA 30342

190

Interesting articles and ads for robots and materials and uses can be found in this magazine.

MOTION
2030 Hillman Circle
Orange, CA 92667

Motion has articles dealing with servo controlled motors and robotic equipment.

MACHINE BLUE BOOK
Hitchcock Building,
Wheaton, IL 60188

Articles on machines, manufacturing and the uses of computers in this environment are the main bulk of this book.

ASSEMBLY ENGINEERING
Hitchcock Building,
Wheaton, IL 60188

This magazine, Machine Blue Book, Quality and 6 others are all published by the Hitchcock Publishing Company. This magazine has some very good articles on new ideas in assembly technology.

ELECTRI-ONICS
17730 W. Peterson Rd.
Libertyville, IL 60048

Excellent articles on circuit board assembly, surface mount technology and testing can be found in this magazine. This company also publishes HYBRID CIRCUIT TECHNOLOGY, MICROELECTRONIC MANUFACTURING AND TESTING and CONNECTION TECHNOLOGY.

ELECTRONIC PRODUCTS
645 Stewart Av.
Garden City, NY 11530

Published twice a month by the Hearst Business Communications company, this magazine has excellent articles on new products, methods of assembly and new technology.

ELECTRONIC PACKAGING & PRODUCTION
P.O. BOX 5690
Denver, CO 80217

This is another of the 32 Cahners publications. It has very good articles on systems, product technology and electronic production.

PRODUCTION ENGINEERING
1111 Chester Av.
Cleveland, OH 44114

Articles on all phases of manufacturing and new technologies are found in this magazine published by the Penton Publishing Company, who also publishes MACHINE DESIGN and several other trade magazines.

RESEARCH AND DEVELOPMENT
Circulation Dept.
Box 5365
New York, NY 10150

This magazine publishes articles on all phases of research and development, science, technologies, computers, manufacturing and materials.

NASA TECH BRIEFS
Technology Transfer Div.
P.O. Box 8757
Baltimore/Washington Airport, MD 21240

This magazine is prepared under the sponsorship of NASA. It lists and describes new inventions and discoveries made by various NASA laboratories. They have done research on just about everything imaginable. Many of the patents are available to the public. Your taxes have helped pay for this research. This magazine demonstrates to some extent what is being done.

BARCODE NEWS
174 Concord St.
Peterborough, NH 03458

Articles devoted to bar code products, technology and its utilization are contained in this magazine.

There are many other good specialized magazines. Once you subscribe to some of the above, you will probably be offered subscriptions to others.

Some are highly technical and a bit dry, but there is a little bit to be learned from each of them. It is one of the better ways to try to keep current with today's lightning-paced technology.

Glossary

Glossary

Access Time—The amount of time it takes the computer to find and read data from a disk or from memory.

Adaptor Boards or Cards—The plug-in boards needed to drive monitors.

Algorithm—A step-by-step procedure, scheme, formula or method used to solve a problem or accomplish a task. May be a subroutine in a software program.

Alphanumeric—Data that has both numerals and letters.

Analyst—A person who determines the computer facilities needed to accomplish a given task. The job of an analyst is similar to that of a consultant. Note that there are no standard qualifications requirements for either of these jobs. Anyone can call themselves an analyst or a consultant. They should be experts in their field, but may not be.

ANSI—American National Standard Institute. A standard adopted by MS-DOS for cursor positioning. It is used in the ANSI.SYS file for device drivers.

ASCII—American Standard Code for Information Interchange. Binary numbers from 0 to 127 that represent the upper and lower case letters of the alphabet, the numbers 0-9 and the several symbols found on a keyboard. A block of eight 0's and 1's are used to represent all of these characters. The first 32 characters, 0-31, are reserved for non-character functions of a keyboard, modem, printer or other device. Number 32, or 00100000, represents the space, which is a character. The numeral one is represented by the binary number for 49, which is 00110001.

Text written in ASCII is displayed on the computer screen as standard text. Text written in other systems, such as WordStar, have several other characters added and are very difficult to read, except through the word processor that created them.

Another 128 character representations has been added to the original 128 for graphics and programming purposes.

ASIC—An acronym for Application Specific Integrated Circuit.

Assembly Language—A low level language of commands that directly manipulate the memory and registers of the computer. It is not as easy to learn as a higher level language such as Pascal or BASIC, and one line of BASIC may perform what one page of assembly language can perform. The advantages of assembly language are vastly better speed, and lower memory and disk space requirements. Once an assembly language program is processed by an *assembler*, it is in the form of 1s and 0s that can be directly understood by the CPU, but before that, it is in the form of short, two or three letter commands written in an ASCII file.

Asynchronous—A serial type of communication where one bit at a time is transmitted. The bits are usually sent in blocks of eight 0s and 1s.

AUTOEXEC.BAT—If present, this file is run automatically by DOS after it boots up. It is a file that can load and run certain programs, or configure your system.

.BAK files—Any time that you edit or change a file in some of the word processors and other software programs they will save the original file as a backup and append the extension .BAK to it.

BASIC—Beginners All Purpose Symbolic Instruction Code. A high level language that was once very popular. There are still many programs and games that use it. It comes standard on the IBM as BASICA. Some of it is in ROM.

Batch—Batch files can be used to link commands and run them automatically. Batch files can be made up easily by the user. They all have the extension .BAT.

Baud—A measurement of the speed or data transfer rate of a communications line between the computer and printer, modem or another computer. Most present day modems operate at 1200 baud. This is 1200 bits per second or 150 characters per second, since each character is a byte, or eight bits long.

Benchmark—A standard program against which similar programs can be compared.

Bidirectional—Both directions. Most printers print in both directions, thereby saving the time it takes to return to the other end of a line.

Binary—Binary numbers are 0s and 1s.

BIOS—An acronym for Basic Input Output System. The BIOS is responsible for handling the input output operations.

Bits—Binary digits. A contraction of Binary and digits.

Boot or Bootstrap—When a computer is turned on, all the memory and other internal operators have to be set or configured. The IBM takes quite a while to boot up because it checks all the memory parity and most of the peripherals. A small amount of the program to do this is stored in ROM. Using this the computer "pulls itself up by its bootstraps." A warm boot is sometimes necessary to get the computer out of an endless loop, or if it is hungup for some reason. A warm boot can be done by pressing Ctrl, Alt and Del.

Bubble Memory—A non volatile type of memory that is created by the magnetization of small bits of ferrous material. It held a lot of promise at one time, but it is rather expensive to make, and it is slower than semiconductor memory.

Buffer—A buffer is usually some discrete amount of memory that is used to hold data. A computer can send data thousands of times faster than a printer or modem can utilize it, but in many cases the computer can do nothing else until all of the data has been transferred. The data can be input to a buffer, which can then feed the data into the printer as needed. The computer is then freed to do other tasks.

Bug, Debug—The early computers were made with high voltage vacuum tubes. It took rooms full of hot tubes to do the job that a credit card calculator can do today. One of the large systems went down one day. After several hours of troubleshooting, the technicians found a large bug that had crawled into the high voltage wiring. It had been electrocuted, but had shorted out the whole system. Since that time any type of trouble in a piece of software or hardware is called a bug. To debug it, of course, is to try to find all of the errors or defects.

Bulletin Boards—Usually a computer with a hard disk that can be accessed with modem. Software and programs can be uploaded or left on the bulletin board by a caller, or a caller can scan the software that has been left there by others and download any that he likes. The BBs often have help and message services. A great source of help for a beginner.

Bus—Wires or circuits that connect a number of devices together. It can also be a system. The IBM PC bus is the configuration of the circuits that connect the 62 pins of the 8 slots together on the mother board. It has become the de facto standard for the clones and compatibles.

Byte—A byte is eight bits, or a block of eight 0s and 1s. These eight bits can be arranged in 256 different ways. This is $2 \times 2 \times 2 \times 2 \times 2 \times 2 \times 2 \times 2 = 256$ or 2 to the eighth power. Therefore, one byte can be made to represent any one of the 256 characters in the ASCII character set. It takes one byte to make a single character.

Cache Memory—A high speed buffer set up to hold data that is being read or written to disks.

Cell—A place for a single unit of data in memory, or an address in a spreadsheet.

Centronics Parallel Port—A system of eight bit parallel transmission first used by the Centronics company. It has become a standard and is the default method of printer output on the IBM.

Character—A letter, a number or an eight bit piece of data.

Chip—An integrated circuit, usually made from a silicon wafer. It can be microscopically etched and have thousands of transistors and semiconductors in a very small area. The 80286 CPU used in the AT has an internal main surface of about one half inch. It has 120,000 transistors on it.

Clock—The operations of a computer are based on very critical timing. So they use a crystal to control their internal clocks. The standard frequency for the PC and XT is 4.77 million cycles per second, or million Hertz. The turbo systems operate at 6 to 8 MHz.

Cluster—Two or more sectors on a track of a disk. Each track of a floppy disk is divided into sectors.

Composite Video—A less expensive monitor that combines all the colors in a single input line.

Console—In the early days a monitor and keyboard was usually set up at a desk like a console. The term has stuck. The console is the keyboard and screen. The command COPY CON allows you to use the keyboard as a typewriter. Enter COPY CON PRN or COPY CON LPT1 and everything you type will be sent to the printer. At the end of your file, or letter, type **Ctrl Z** or **F6** to stop sending.

Consultant—Someone who is supposed to be an expert who can advise and help you determine what your computer needs are. Similar to an analyst. There are no standard requirements or qualifications that must be met. So anyone can call themselves an analyst or consultant.

Coprocessor—Usually an 8087 or 80287 chip that works in conjunction with the CPU and vastly speeds up mathematical operations.

Copy Protection—A system that prevents a diskette from being copied.

CPU—Central Processing Unit such as the 8088 or 80286 chips.

Current Directory—The directory that is in use at the time.

Cursor—The blinking spot on the screen that indicates where next character will be input.

Daisy Wheel—A round printer or typewriter wheel with flexible fingers that have the alphabet and other formed characters.

Database—A collection of data, usually related in some way, such as a series of records of name, address, phone number, job title, and salary.

DATE Command—Date will be displayed anytime DATE is typed at the prompt sign.

Documentation—Manuals, instructions or specifications for a system, hardware or software.

Double Density—At one time, most diskettes were single sided, and had a capacity of 80 to 100 K. Then the capacity was increased and technology was advanced so that the the diskettes could be recorded on both sides with up to 200 K per side double sided, double density. Then quad density was soon introduced with 400 K per side. Then came the newer 1.6 Mb high density diskettes. All of the above figures are before formatting. Most double density is the common 360 K formatted. The quad ends up with 720 K formatted and the high density is 1.2 Mb.

Dumb Terminal—A terminal that is tied to a mainframe or one that does not have its own microprocessor.

ECHO—A batch file command that causes information to be displayed on the screen.

EEPROM—An Electrically Erasable Programmable Read Only Memory chip.

EPROM—An Erasable Programmable Read Only Memory chip.

Ergonomics—The study and science of how the human body can be the most productive in working with machinery. This would include the study of the effects of things like the type of monitor, the type of chair, lighting and other environmental and physical factors.

Errors—DOS displays several error messages if it receives bad commands or there are problems of some sort.

Expansion Boards—Boards that can be plugged into one of the slots on the mother board to add memory or other functions.

External Commands—DOS commands that are not loaded into memory when the computer is booted.

FAT—An acronym for the File Allocation Table. This is a table on the disk that DOS uses to keep track of all of the parts of a file. A file may be placed in sector 3 of track one, sectors 5 and 6 of track ten and sector 4 of track 20. The File Allocation Table would keep track of where they are and will direct the read or record head to those areas.

Fonts—The different types of print letters such as Gothic, Courier, Roman, Italic and others.

Fragmentation—If a diskette has several records that have been changed several times, there are bits of the files on several different tracks and sectors. This slows down writing and reading of the files because the head has to move back and forth to the various tracks. If these files are copied to a newly formatted diskette, each file will be written to clean tracks that are contiguous. This will decrease the access time to the diskette or hard disk.

Friction Feed—A printer that uses a roller or platen to pull the paper through.

Game Port—An Input/Output (I/O) port for joysticks, trackballs, paddles and other devices.

Gigabyte—One billion bytes. This will probably be a common size memory in a very short time.

Glitch—An unexpected electrical spike or static disturbance that can cause loss of data. Also known as a *gremlin*.

Global—An operation or search that is performed through an entire document or program.

Handshaking—A protocol or routine between systems, usually the printer and the computer, to indicate readiness to communicate with each other.

Hexadecimal—A numbering system that uses the base 16. The binary system is based on 2, our decimal system is based on 10. The hexadecimal digits are 0, 1, 2, 3, 4, 5, 6, 7, 8, 9, A, B, C, D, E, F. 10 hex would be 16 decimal, and 20 hex would be 32 in decimal. Most of the memory locations are in hexadecimal notation.

Hidden Files—The files that do not show up in a normal directory display.

High Level Language—A language such as BASIC, Pascal, or C. These program languages are fairly easy to read and understand.

ICs—Integrated Circuits. The first integrated circuit was the placing of two transistors in a single can early in the 1960s. Soon, ways were found to put several semiconductors in a package. It was called SSI, or Small Scale Integration. Then LSI, or Large Scale Integration, then VLSI or Very Large Scale Integration. Today we have VHSIC or Very High Scale Integrated Circuits. We have almost run out of descriptive adjectives.

Interface—A piece of hardware or a set of rules that allows communications between two systems.

Internal Commands—Those commands that are loaded into memory when DOS boots up.

Interpreter—A program that translates a high level language into machine readable code.

Kilobyte—1000 bytes, or more exactly, 1024 bytes. This is 2 to the 10th power. Often abbreviated 1 K.

LAN—An acronym for Local Area Network where several computers might be tied together or to a central server.

Low-Level Language—A language that is closer to the workings of the computer than it is to the workings of human language. Assembly language is the most common example of a low-level language.

LQ—Letter Quality, the type from a daisy wheel or formed type printers.

Mainframe—A large computer that may serve several users.

Megabyte—1,000,000 bytes, or 1 Mb. More precisely, it is 2 to the 20th power, or 1,048,576 bytes.

Menu—A list of choices or options. A menu driven system makes it very easy for beginners to choose what they want to run or do.

NLQ—An acronym for Near Letter Quality. The better formed characters from a dot-matrix printer.

Null Modem Cable—A cable with certain pairs of wires crossed over. If the computer sends data from pin 2, the modem may receive it on pin 3. The modem would send data back to the computer from its pin 2 and be received by the computer on pin 3. Several other wires would also be crossed.

Parallel—A system that uses 8 lines to send 8 bits at a time.

Plotter—An X-Y writing device that can be used for charts, graphics and many other functions that most printers can't do.

Prompt—The > sign that shows that DOS is waiting for an entry.

RAM—Random Access Memory. A volatile memory. Any data stored in it is lost when the power is turned off.

RGB—For Red, Green and Blue, the three primary colors that are used in color monitors and tvs. Each color has its own electron gun that shoots streams of electrons to the back of the monitor display and causes it to light up in the various colors.

ROM—Read Only Memory. It does not change when the power is turned off.

Sector—A section of a track on a disk or diskette.

Serial—The transmission of one bit at a time over a single line.

Source—The origin, or diskette to be copied from.

Target—The diskette to be copied to.

Time Stamp—The record of the time and date that is recorded in the directory when a file is created or changed.

Tractor—A printer device with sprockets or spikes that pulls the computer paper with the holes in the margins through the printer at a very precise feed rate. A friction feed platen may allow the paper to slip, move to one side or the other, and not be precise in the spacing between the lines.

Turbo—Usually means a computer with a faster than normal speed.

User Friendly—Usually means bigger and more expensive. It should make using the computer easier. Memory is now less expensive, so large programs are being developed to use more memory than ever before.

User Groups—Usually a club or a group of people who use computers. Often the club will be devoted to users of a certain type of computer. Although usually anyone is welcome to join.

Virtual—Something that may be essentially present, but not in actual fact. If you have a single disk drive, it will be drive A, but you also have a virtual drive B if your DIP switches on the mother board are set properly.

Windows—Many new software packages are now loaded into memory. They stay in the background until they are called for, then they will pop up on the screen in a window. The thesaurus program, Word-Finder, is such a program. If I want a synonym for a word, I press Ctrl and F6 and a window opens over the top of my text with a list of words. It does not disturb the text that I was working on and quickly allows me to continue.

Index

Index

Edited by Carl D. Aron

Other Bestsellers From TAB

☐ **80386—A PROGRAMMING AND DESIGN HAND-BOOK—Penn Brumm and Don Brumm**

The basis of IBM's much-anticipated OS/2 operating system and their new Personal System/2 computers, the 80386 microprocessor promises new standards in microcomputer power, speed, and versatility. Now, with the cooperation of 80386 designers from Intel Corporation, Penn and Don Brumm have provided the first complete sourcebook on this advanced processor, including an overview of its capabilities and in-depth information for programmers and designers. 448 pp., 97 illus.

Paper $19.95   **Hard $29.95**
Book No. 2937

☐ **POWER PROGRAMMING WITH ADA® FOR THE IBM PC®—John Winters, Ph.D.**

This excellent new guide puts Ada programming within easy understanding. Whether you'd simply like to find out how Ada works or you need a fundamental knowledge of Ada to compete more effectively in the Defense Department-related marketplace, John Winters leads you easily and effectively through the principles of Ada programming from step one to actual program writing. He even includes an extensive glossary filled with sample code that's an ideal programming reference. 220 pp., 153 illus.

Paper $16.95   **Hard $24.95**
Book No. 2902

☐ **ENCYCLOPEDIA OF LOTUS® 1-2-3® A COMPLETE CROSS-REFERENCE TO ALL MACROS, COMMANDS, FUNCTIONS, APPLICATIONS AND TROUBLE-SHOOTING—Robin Stark**

Now, at last, there is one single sourcebook that can answer *all* your questions about Lotus 1-2-3—from the basics of installing this popular, general-purpose business software on your IBM PC or compatible, to advanced applications data; from a listing of commands and functions to the most efficient use of macros; and from user tips and shortcuts to troubleshooting techniques. It fully describes and gives working examples for *all* of the commands, subcommands, functions, and macro tools found in the latest version of 1-2-3. 496 pp., 183 illus.

Paper $19.95   **Hard $29.95**
Book No. 2891

☐ **THE dBASE III® PLUS PROGRAMMER'S REFERENCE—A SOURCEBOOK OF PROGRAMMING TECHNIQUES—Cary N. Prague and James E. Hammitt**

This indispensible guide covers all the improved, advanced features of dBASE III® PLUS, including over 50 new programming commands, the ability to open up to 10 files at once, a screen painter, and Advanced Query System, and an Assist mode. 240 pp., 150 illus.

Paper $18.95   **Book No. 2856**

☐ **CLIPPER™: dBASE® COMPILER APPLICATIONS—Gary Beam**

Going well beyond the standard user's manual, this book provides you with a treasury of programming techniques and applications examples that allows you to take maximum advantage of Clipper's program development potential. Whether you are a novice Clipper user in need of hands-on guidance in mastering this dBASE the compiler's many special functions and features or an experienced program developer looking for new techniques to enhance your programming efficiency, this book is a must. 190 pp., 37 illus.

Paper $16.95   **Book No. 2917**

☐ **PROGRAMMING WITH R:BASE® SYSTEM V—Cary N. Prague, James E. Hammitt, and Allan P. Thompson**

The first complete guide to tapping all the multifaceted features of R:BASE System V, allowing you to achieve maximum speed, versatility, and power no matter what your current or future application needs might be. Whether you're trying to get a better grasp of how R:BASE System V works, want some advanced programming tips to add power and productivity to your programming or just want to know more about this DBMS before making a purchase . . . you won't be disappointed in this excellent new book. 400 pp., 416 illus.

Paper $19.95   **Hard $29.95**
Book No. 2896

☐ **ADVANCED PROGRAMMING WITH dBASE III® PLUS—Cary N. Prague and James E. Hammitt**

This sequel to Prague and Hammitt's bestselling *Programming with dBASE III PLUS* leads you through all of the advanced new features offered by dBASE, with even greater emphasis on the use of macros and other power programming techniques. You'll learn how to use your software's improved options to produce more impressive looking screens and reports and to handle more sophisticated database applications with ease. 352 pp., 262 illus.

Paper $19.95   **Hard $24.95**
Book No. 2876

☐ **C PROGRAMMER'S UTILITY LIBRARY—Frank Whitsell**

Here's a sourcebook that goes beyond simple programming techniques to focus on the efficient use of system resources to aid in the development of higher quality C programs! It's a unique collection of ready-to-use functions and utilities ranging from control modules for your video display and keyboard to times for more fully tapping the power of DOS and taking control of your PC's asynchronous communications ports! 200 pp., 268 illus.

Paper $16.95   **Hard $24.95**
Book No. 2855

Other Bestsellers From TAB

☐ **WORKING WITH FOCUS®: AN INTRODUCTION TO DATABASE MANAGEMENT—Clifford A. Schaffer**

Every aspect of this powerful, business-oriented software system is covered . . . from building and entering a database, the parts of FOCUS, and the format of data fields to entering data, FOCUS reports, and more. 256 pp., 91 illus.

Paper $22.95   **Book No. 2810**

☐ **PRODOS® INSIDE AND OUT—Dennis Doms and Tom Weishaar**

This introduction to programming with BASIC SYSTEM gives practical tips and how-to advice on everything from booting your system to assembly language programming with ProDOS. You'll even cover such hard-to-find topics as subdirectories and their use, programming examples for the Field and Byte options of text files, the use of BSAVE and BLOAD parameters to save disk space, and more! 270 pp., 113 illus.

Paper $16.95   **Hard $24.95**
Book No. 2745

☐ **THE ILLUSTRATED HANDBOOK OF DESKTOP PUBLISHING AND TYPESETTING—Michael L. Kleper**

"The encyclopedic work on the subject"—**Personal Publishing Magazine.** Now, here's the first comprehensive analysis of desktop publishing by one of the nation's top authorities in this emerging field! 784 pp., 615 illus.

Paper $29.95   **Hard $49.95**
Book No. 2700

☐ **LOTUS® 1-2-3® SIMPLIFIED—2nd Edition, Including Version 2.0—David Bolocan**

The ideal book to guide you painlessly from the most basic computer and spreadsheet operations right through the most advanced and powerful operations of 2.0! 272 pp., 207 illus.

Paper $14.95   **Hard $21.95**
Book No. 2748

☐ **MASTERING SYMPHONY®—2nd Edition—David Bolocan**

Here's an up-to-date look at Symphony, including Version 1.1, that even novice users of the IBM® PC, PC-XT®, or PC-compatible machines can follow with ease. The author approaches his topic in such a logical way that it's like having guidance from a private consultant. 240 pp., 238 illus.

Paper $16.95   **Hard $22.95**
Book No. 2718

☐ **PROGRAMMING WITH R:base® 5000—Cary N. Prague and James E. Hammitt**

Picking up where user's manuals leave off, Prague and Hammitt guide you through all the many capabilities offered by R:base 5000, and show you how to adapt these capabilities for your own applications needs. In fact, the authors cover everything from how to use basic R:base tools to using R:base 5000 as a complete programming language for writing your own applications programs. 400 pp., 266 illus.

Paper $19.95   **Hard $28.95**
Book No. 2666

*Prices subject to change without notice.